VALUES
AND THE
CREDIBILITY OF
THE PROFESSOR

Louis William Norris
President Emeritus of Albion College

University Press
of America™

Library of Congress Catalog Card Number: 80-5501

To
Faculty Colleagues
from whom I have learned much

TABLE OF CONTENTS

PREFACE

Learning consists in grasping a subject that has import of good or ill, indifference or consequence, for the learner. It generates values of varying quality superior to ignorance whenever and wherever undertaken. This book seeks to show that every professor, not merely those traditionally committed to "value studies," is involved in proposing some values through teaching. Credibility of each professor comprises the value import of what is offered to students.

It would be a repetitious "idiot debate" to consider again whether education does or should include concern with values, as Max Lerner points out in his excellent manual on Values in Education.[1] The crucial question relates to the valuational role of each professor in the teaching process itself. It is the credibility gap that has widened between professors and their students, as well as the general public, that calls for new attention to the values in their work.

No mere revival of "moral education" is called for here, much as many parents and other citizens wish the academic community would set their students straight. Values do motivate and result from conduct, and, therefore, the import of a college education for moral values is plentiful. But bodily, economic, aesthetic, social, religious, logical, political, and now environmental values, are also part of every person's life. A student's curriculum will touch each of these and other values in one way or another. It is this wide-ranging life of value and the professor's role in it that is our theme.

Another study of which professors are now widely believed would also be superfluous. A popular professor is easily detected and not always respected by his peers. We have enough "studies" and statistics about "what's happening" in education to last awhile. How to increase listeners needs no more messiahs, for

---

[1] Phi Delta Kappa Education Foundation: Bloomington, Indiana, 1976, p. 13.

v

the tonnage of volumes on how-to-do-it and the yen for experimentation are already prolific. Credibility remains the heart of acceptance by students. But the question that must be attended to is when the professor deserves to be believed.

A professor, even the most extreme nihilist, would be hard to find who would deny that values are "something or other" with which men and women have to do. But those who have worked through the import of values in learning, and therefore in teaching their subject, are dismayingly few. Most professors, like everybody else, believe values "have their place," that each person has his own values, and has a right to deal with them as he chooses. But the conflict of values in American democracy, and the hodge-podge of values teeming on the typical college campus, make such a laissez-faire attitude toward values no longer tolerable. A new effort to clear the blurred picture of learning by the tuning device of value is in order.

What makes such a venture particularly pertinent now is the recession in higher education that has attended the economic recession of the 1970s, following boom years in academia during the '60s. It manifests itself in the attitudes of professors, their students and general public.

For professors "the trauma of self-doubt" has made sober inroads into their work. The surveys of 4400 professors on 161 campuses by Seymour Lipset and Everett Ladd, Jr., report a "pervasive mood of pessimism," and a striking lack of "confidence in the efficacy of the institution" in which they serve. Some 61% have considered leaving the academic world in the period of 1975-1977.[2] Far from overwhelming professors with their open-mouthed belief, many students are inclined toward a numbness that makes college a "holding operation," a haven of "least hassle." Recent Carnegie and Newman reports show academic institutions pulled in contrary directions, when not neglected, and a "crisis of confidence" in

---

[2] Reported in The Chronicle of Higher Education, xi: 16 (Jan. 12, 1976), p. 14. The Washington Post, Jan. 3, 1978, Sec. A, pp. 1, 5.

higher education by the general public.[3]

No doubt every age is considered a crisis in
some sense. This one is the best informed in history. But the unease remarked on every hand is
about what matters, what values should be made
central. Academia with its superior staff in intellect and training is needed to settle or at
least clarify such questions, perhaps even more
than to supply the additional information, which
is largely the thrust of its present research.

While the private and church-related colleges
never had a corner on value studies, their decline
in proportionate numbers of students enrolled can
mean a considerable loss to the quality of American life. Such sectarianism, separateness and
elitism as many of them represented have been
largely diluted by law and public opinion. But
after the elimination of chapel services, required
courses in religion and parietal rules, these colleges could well retain the vitality and centrality
of value considerations, which the Hebrew-Christian
tradition emphasized.

"What does it profit a man, if he gain the
whole world. . ." needs to be a prior and persisting question in all learning. Sensitivity to differing people and the demands of justice, as well
as mercy in pursuit of the common good are problems
for every man. They are the obligations of membership in the human race. The small colleges, especially those with church interest and support,
have a continuing mission to nurture the conscience
of the nation. But whatever the type of educational
institution, its mission must include articulation
and coherence among the values which learning implies and scholarship makes possible.

John Stuart Mill's fears for the future of
democracy, based on the observation that the better
people are informed the harder they are to lead,
need to be taken to heart. The capacity of the pub-

---

[3]David Mathews, "Carnegie and Newman: Higher Education in Traction." Saturday Review/World, 1:11
(Feb. 9, 1974), p. 64.

lic to understand media reports on budgets, figures
about the gross national product, balance of trade
problems, space flight logistics, medical treatments,
environmental trends, racial conflicts and political
scandals is remarkable. But help in decision about
values that should guide solution to the problems
these reports bear is what lags. Unless democracy
can articulate its values as a political system and
coordinate its many interests it will remain vulner-
able to totalitarian self-promotion and aggrandize-
ment. But a coordination, that would not repeat the
monolithic solidarity of authoritarian government,
would be possible only if the valuational competence
of citizens could be relied on. Where else could
such competence come from more reliably than from
professors?

Educators cannot claim legitimately that the
values that count will rise to the top if they would
only be listened to. Traditional conceptions of
higher education, and hence of the professor's work,
have obviously not been doing the job, and a sober
number of professors realize it. Yet many books on
teaching go on assuming that professors have only
to be appreciated and all will be well. Gilbert
Highet's The Immortal Profession, The Joys of Teaching and Learning makes such an assumption.[4] But it
fails to grasp the threat of internal decay and external attack that the values of western civilization
face. These cultural threats stem from the fate of
values in which each professor should have a major
stake.

It is with the internal causes of the recession
in higher education that we must be concerned. These
causes stem from the negligence that values in learning have been allowed. What matters most to the
humanity of human beings and their social organizations has simply not been given the systematic attention which learning by its very nature should comment upon. What scholarship when taken to be "good
enough" says about the values of the learner who accepts them must be made more clear. This means that
what one "truth" has to do with another must be shown

---

[4]New York: Weybright and Tolley, Inc., 1977.

by those who hold it, and not left to fend for itself. "Our final obligation is not to the truth. . .
but to the people who need the truth," as Meiklejohn
liked to emphasize.

With the onrush of new knowledge and the rise
of specialized studies, the complex curriculum and
elective courses have put a high premium on fragmentary learning. Professors have welcomed freedom
from their nineteenth century role as drillmasters
of agreed upon classic common elements in the curriculum. They have responded with zest to "exploration" as the work of a scholar. Max Weber's pontification that ". . .Nothing is worthy of a man unless he can pursue it with passionate devotion"
and with "blinders" from distracting consideration,[5]
has become a golden text for many an American
professor.

Life as we live it, however, and hence its
values as we experience them, is not a succession
of fragmentary states of awareness. It is a flow-
ing complex of forces qualified by factors of in-
numberable character. Coals taken from the fire
go out. The meaning and value of fragmentary, highly
specialized knowledge suffer from their segregation,
unless the origin, kinship, family membership and
import of such segregation is made known.

No one can doubt the pertinence of specialized
knowledge for our complex and specialized society.
But "What ultimate good is it?" remains a haunting
question to every scholar. Specialized knowledge
is easier to obtain than "a broader outlook,"
where values are continuously attended to. Can
scholars be content with criteria of excellence
for their work which merely gauge what is most
easily done? Henry James gained eminence for his
"artistic purity," yet H. G. Wells observed that he
betrayed the human race by such preciousness.[6]

---

[5]From Max Weber (Tr. Hans Gerth and C. Wright Mills).
New York: Oxford University Press, 1946, p. 135.

[6]Martin Green, "The Visible College in British Science." The American Scholar, 47:1 (Winter, 1977-
78), p. 106.

Though Wells' judgment of James was probably unfair, his call for a symmetry of values was pertinent. It is time to consider whether scholarship by its isolationism is betraying the human race.

If there were only one crevice in our culture, that between the two cultures of science and humanism stressed by C. P. Snow, how fortunate we would be. But it is the fiefdoms of separate disciplines in academe, the ghettoes of economic, ethnic, intellectual, and spiritual clusters in our society that divide us. It is not that no one cares about values. What wears down our hopes and frays our nerves is the bungling way in which value questions are so often treated.

Fear of involvement in value questions by sincere and conscientious scholars usually implies belief that values are vague and subjective, separable from facts and "verifiable" observations. These reactions, it is time to admit, must be taken only to state the problems of value, and to reflect inability or unwillingness to wrestle with them. For even to pursue truth in any form is to assert value in doing it. Even if answers to value questions were to remain forever inexact, and many need not do so, they would still affect what professors take to be true.

Some answers to value questions do remain inexact, like the merits of democracy, virtues of religion, proportion of good and evil in nature's influence, the role of conscience. Yet every man tries to answer them and acts as if he could assume a reliable answer to them. We proceed through life with inexact answers to questions of importance while we seek to make each answer more exact.

What is basic is that questions of value be continuously asked and pursued relentlessly. Gertrude Stein's dying words, "What's the question?" remain the pertinent issue of scholarship, as of life itself. This book concerns the questions professors pursue, and maintains that the value

questions are the ultimate and crucial ones. The
politics of ideas, that is, the processes by which
ideas are adopted, are as important as the concepts
or insights they contain. Such acceptance as good
enough for adoption is a matter of values.

Basic questions for which answers are sought
here would occur to most anyone who takes seriously
the role of values in teaching. How are values to
be defined? What bearing does the role of valuer
in knowledge have on the professor's conception of
his own identity or vocation? In what ways do the
functions of the institution in which the professor
labors figure in solving value problems? To what
extent does a professor's scheme of values affect
his interpretation of and preparation for the future?
How are values to be judged as reliable and in what
ways can a professor develop value competence?

Competition among values on the campus is so
often a tug-of-war between opposites. Where do
freedom and authority, bodily needs and moral duties,
personal and social welfare, material and mental, as
well as spiritual, possessions shade into or cancel
out each other? Competent counsel that is more than
that of a referee is needed. As the pragmatists
and rationalists, materialists, liberals and con-
servatives, puritans and libertarians, battle for
converts no one camp can at present elevate itself
to self-evident authority.

Can the ultimate service of a professor be more
notable than to provide some value calculus to un-
scramble and to relate those polarities where they
can be established? This supreme function of a
credible professor is more than skill in setting
forth arguments "on the one hand," while steam
builds up for views "on the other hand." The tensions among values call for such a means of accommodation as is irreducible to any one combatant, and
requisite of no further test for its efficacy. Is
there any more credible value capable of dealing
with the others?

It will not do to blame the preponderance of
oppositions in daily life on the proclivity of Western thought to arrange things in Aristotelian cate-

gories standing in "substantial" distinction and opposition to each other. Nor can we suppose that the sophisticated dialectic of theses, antitheses and syntheses of Hegel, partially adopted by Marxians, accounts for the "over againstness" of many forces we confront. These tensions are in the raw experience of human persons and are to be reconciled in the struggle for psychologically mature personhood and civilized culture. Dewey's effort to merge thought and action, value and fact, growth and reflection, needs a more articulate calculus for polarity. Here is the crux of a professor's credibility.

It is sometimes said that any reflection on education is a venture in autobiography. Consequently, I should add that concern for the role of values in learning has been a preoccupation for me since college days. After fifteen years as a professor of philosophy, and nearly twenty-five years as a college administrator and government officer disbursing funds to support education in the humanities, the crucial function of professors in identifying and nurturing the values in our culture has, in my judgment, ever grown in certainty. The professor's task is not only to bail his generation out of trouble, but to lead it to such values as will enlarge the humanity in man.

No parochial priest of a favorite set of values, the responsible professor nonetheless recognizes his purveyance of value by teaching. He labors with as many intellectual blisters to find and make clear the inevitable values in his discipline as he does to find the facts, formulae, processes, methods, and social norms of conventional scholarship. He helps students discover "what they are getting into" by learning. In so doing he helps students eventually to answer their show-down question, "So what?"

In addition to many a lively discussion with professors and administrators at Albion College and George Washington University, I have had the privilege of conference with hundreds of professors from many parts of the country, while serving as a program officer with the National Endowment for the Humanities. There are signs of promise as some

colleges, universities and professional schools
are coming to see that "experiments" and "new
methods" will not regain the integrity of their
institutions, and hence the credibility of their
professors. It's the value import of their
teaching that determines when education is "good
enough," and when professors deserve credibility.

Washington, D. C.   Louis William Norris

CHAPTER ONE

WHEN GODOT COMES

I

When and for what reasons should a student believe in his professors? As the tide of approval and support ebbs and flows around schools and colleges, the lighthouse that beams brightly or flickers faintly is the credibility of professors. Foreboding heard on many sides about the grave "legitimacy crisis" in education today deprecates this credibility. Such fears do not fall gently on my mind, as they surely may not for any responsible educator.

About the last piece of advice given me by one of my graduate professors, who knew I was about to become an instructor in philosophy, was, "Remember, they'll believe what you say." It was meant to be a reminder that I must be fully prepared before I ventured to teach a single class. But I have come to realize that those students who don't believe what the professor says are the ones he must be even more concerned about. From these students comes the evidence sometimes of their valid critical powers, but more often of their failure to be convinced of their professors' credibility.

Perhaps the most telling feature of our Western industrialized culture is the "alienation" it reflects, not merely of the economically dispossessed, but of the privileged also. And this goes for students too. It is an "uncommitted" generation. Many in it are preoccupied with the "Exorcist" art of distortion, novels of violence and unfulfillment, especially of sex, like Kosinski's The Painted Bird, and music that is discordant and blindly emotional. The quality of human life does not seem to be improving, so one should not "get involved." With no clear vision of a good and attainable future, the best strategy is to keep your guard up.[1]

---

[1] Cf. Kenneth Keniston, The Uncommitted. New York: Harcourt, Brace & World, 1965, pp. 3-20, 455-464.

Even students, and there are many, who are not inclined to rebel against the academic community, their parents, or their society, soon discover the down-beat, splintering, and destructive nature of the off-campus world they will soon enter. They are bound to look to their professors, designated pace-setters of their society, to see what is worthy of their efforts. They can't help asking whether their professors have answers that command their energy and hopes.

We cannot, of course, hold professors primarily responsible for the splitting up of society into the specialized, technologically guided milieu it has become. The fragmented and atomistic character of much scholarship does feed such a segmented society, thus fostering its disintegrating forces and hindering the coherent self-direction of its citizens. But the antagonisms of special groups, the self-defeating conflicts of the never-satisfied affluent, the disparities in opportunity between ethnic groups, geographical areas, and differing nationalities have many far-ranging origins.

If any composure, growth in culture, or social progress is to come, however, we must know which alternatives count most. Such learning is the professor's business. Lyndon Johnson's plaintive description of his work is a symbol of Everyman. "The problem of the presidency," he said, "is not so much in doing what is right as knowing what is right." To the leaders of "the knowledge industry," the professors, we may legitimately look for answers to what is right for us to know. With the overwhelming majority of influence-makers college educated, the fate of our culture is more than ever in the hands of professors. Can they supply us with values that supplant alienation with a vibrant equilibrium? Is not this coherence in values through learning what lies behind the more superficial student cry for "relevance?"

Socrates' query of Hippocrates concerning his teacher, Protagoras, "What is he and what will he make of you?"[2] is one every professor should try

---

[2] Protagoras, 311B.

2

to answer each morning before going to work. What values in knowing the discipline that will be set before students that day are the reasons for teaching? Determination of what these values are is half the professor's problem. The other half concerns their believability by students, if teaching is to succeed. It is both the competence of professors to deal with value, and the withdrawal of the endorsement by students, as well as the public, that are at issue in this fragmented generation.

II

After the swell of institutional growth, with its attendant expectation of optimal solutions to almost any problem in the early '60s, the tide today is running out. The retreat from education, at least as traditionally conceived, is manifested not only by this dismaying alienation of many students despite their "eerie quietude." It shows also in the growing reluctance of parents to pay higher fees and legislatures to expand support of educational institutions.[3] Peter Drucker's prediction that over half the gross national product will be plowed into "the knowledge industry" by 1980 does not promise fulfillment.

Repudiation of higher education per se is not so much the vogue, though there is evidence of that too, as the willingness, even demand, that it pay off in relatively immediate and materially measurable

---

[3] Fred Hechinger, former education editor of the New York Times, holds that this retreat amounts to "Murder in Academe: The Demise of Education." Such a "festering doubt about education" threatens, he believes, the very "survival of American Democracy," for it marks a withdrawal from preparation of the country's cultural and political leaders as well as their responsible followers. Saturday Review, 3:12 (March 20, 1976), p. 11.

consequences. Stress is on career education, the "academic revolution" identified by Riesman and Jencks, specialization, economic success, innovation, efficiency, and "rights" to equality of accomplishment. Unless the professor makes a convincing contribution to these ends his credibility is in jeopardy. Belief in other values usually considered essential to the educated person is either ignored or subject to searing debate.

While the demand for short range "practical" results has challenged education as any broad cultural and intellectual quality in every generation, its intensity is heightened by this period's questioning of values on nearly every front. Abraham Maslow went so far as to say that, ". . .all the traditional systems of value ever offered to mankind have proved to be failures."[4] Degradation of much traditional language to four-letter words and many visual art forms by pornography raise the question of what form of culture fosters human development most effectively. The values inviting study of a professor's discipline, guiding its methodology and pursuit, as well as those expected from its mastery, are no longer considered self-evident. And if the professor has an "unpopular" discipline, like foreign language or ancient history, what values can count for him?

If the traditional view could be retained, that sound scholarship is "objective" and "value-free," the professor's task would be greatly simplified. He could let his constituents bring their own values to his teaching and make of it what they would. But such freedom from involvement with values is coming more clearly to be perceived as an illusion. The professor who thanked God at the national convention of his mathematics society that his paper had no practical value whatever would now be taken as a mere trifler. A teacher "selects" subjects, applies "best" methods, seeks "important" results, reflects a given "outlook" or "perspective," and strives to turn out "competent" students. Value

---

[4]New Knowledge in Human Values. New York: Harper & Brothers, 1959, p. vii.

judgments infiltrate his every step. His only option is to articulate this inevitability to himself
and his students, and to guard against blatant bias,
personal interest and shoddy axiology.

Credibility involves the work of the professor
and its acceptance as important by students. To
appeal to time, as Schopenhauer did when only a few
students came to his lectures, is a risky business
in this fast-moving age. A successful professor
gains credibility as he is able to persuade students
that his discipline impinges on their scheme of
values in such a way as to enhance what truly matters today, and will with great probability tomorrow.

It is the diversity in valuation of what matters most that makes so poignant the professor's
effort to avoid the "trauma of self-doubt," so
current by the end of the '60s. Many of the other
professions, notably law, medicine and business,
are also gravely concerned that they are not now
loved as they once were. W. H. Auden's characterization of his day as an "age of anxiety" seems to
many even more apt now as threats mount inherent in
nuclear power, overpopulation, scarcity of environmental resources, political violence, crime, mental
disorder and incurable cancer. Not only are old
values questioned. Some new problems leave questions
of value wholly obscure.

The despair, so current in Germany and France
after two World Wars, prompted and sustained the
existentialists, led by Heidegger and Sartre, to
seek answers "out of actual experience." But the
ambiguities, cross-currents, conflicts and uncertainties of "actual experience" are the very matrix
in which the professor must formulate the values he
offers as credible to his students. It is a criterion for values in his experience he needs.

III

As a college administrator I early realized
that the American public has expected its schools
and colleges to come up with reliable criteria of

value. A Gallup poll in 1975 showed that 75% of those participating wanted the schools to deal with moral problems. Sex education has been expected of many schools, or at least some guidance in sex behavior. A similar expectation applies to manners, drugs and alcohol. Most parents have been reluctant to see the "in loco parentis" conception of college life go. The ten million students now pursuing higher education reflect the belief of those supporting them that a college education will "do them good." "Help them amount to something," to be "a good doctor," "a good father," "a good" something, the parents say to deans and presidents.

Much of the value-cultivation, which is the legitimate expectation and, to some extent, exclusive obligation of families, churches and civic community organizations, has been projected on educational institutions. The latter are commonly expected to be the "final fortress" against the disintegration of society's values, and the "residual legatees of social obligation."[5] Teaching is valuing, but the professor can scarcely accept the order to deliver on all values. Many are deep-rooted before students come to college. Others will mature away from the campus.

The social confusion we now confront reveals both that the educational institutions have been expected to do too much, and that there is great division of opinion over what the schools should be expected to do. A professor looking for a valid base on which to rest his credibility will get little help from public judgment. Neither the P. T. A. nor the alumni association can be relied on to tell the teacher what "good" should result from learning. They are too divided and too inflated in their demands.

Divisions in purpose are of dismaying proportions among the professional educators too, as attendance at meetings of the American Council on Education, or of the Association of American Col-

---

[5] Max Lerner, _Values in Education_. Bloomington, Ind.: Phi Delta Kappa Education Foundation, 1976, p. 13.

leges repeatedly will confirm. The professor is left to his own responsibility for a standard of value he cannot avoid, and his students desperately need. Should he line up with those humanists who blame technology and the computer for maiming the early American belief that education would bring the good life? Can he regard the secularization of the schools as the cause of rootlessness in this generation, or should he eschew a Puritan ethic in education as too inflexible for new conditions? Must discipline be reinstated to stem the tide of permissiveness, or would that mean a return to joylessness in learning? Has history anything to teach a counter culture about sex, drugs and direct action? Should the professor's efforts extend to students of all ranges in ability, cultural and academic preparation, or should the most capable be urged forward? Indecision about "which values" is as serious for the credibility of professors as the willingness to shun all value involvement.

Many a student, I fear, finds himself "Waiting for Godot," as the popularity of that play testifies. That Beckett contrives to show that Godot never comes is a sober message. When Lindy is bidden "to think," he only holds forth in gibberish. In the absence of more convincing answers to questions of where his energies should be expended a student's "thinking" spins its wheels. So many only drift, or think of education as a mere means of meeting the necessity to make some kind of a living. Others drop out believing "a good enough living" is obtainable by their own devices unaided by formal education.

A professor establishes his credibility, assisting Godot to come, when he identifies what for many students seems to be left out of learning. It consists in such convincing values as allow experience with nature, other people and the totality of things to be combined into illumination of the human condition and motivation toward meaningful action. It is the conveyance by a professor of import to what may already be known but unappreciated, or what can be learned to have bearing on the character and quality of human life. Its recognition in the "Aha moment" indicates that the study of a subject is making sense.

A skillful professor is a kind of Marcel Marceau doing a pantomime. When Marceau presents "Walking the Dog," his extended hand, jerking, stretching, while he walks slowly, stops, turns around, then moves on, conveys the actions of a dog as vividly as would be possible if the dog were on the stage. What is left out of much teaching is often as important as what is actually taught.

What is crucial is that the implied references are discoverable and worthy of defense. This is to say that the value import of the professor's teaching may be as significant, or even more so, than what he says. A physiological psychologist leaves out the rational functions of the human being, implying that there aren't any. But even his science would then be impossible.

This insertion of real or implied connections, the supplement of isolated factors with context, is the way of showing import even for the most exact science. Thus, the Heisenberg theory of indeterminacy in physics stipulates that an electron may be thought of as a particle. It can be located at a given point in a given instant but you cannot identify the direction or speed of its taking off. Measurement of its speed would, on the other hand, be meaningless without reference to some point. The containment of these variables in the quantum formula supplied by Max Planck allows us to deal with energy intelligibly. It supplies what is missing from actually observed phenomena.[6] The value of these phenomena lies in their meaning, which states the import of the separate happenings.

To say that Lincoln was honest, that Beethoven's Ninth Symphony is great, or that cherry trees blooming in Washington are beautiful, is to fill in what is missing from the sheer reading, hearing, or seeing

---

[6] Cf. Jacob Bronowski, "The Principle of Tolerance," Atlantic, 232:6 (December 1973), pp. 60-66.

8

of these subjects. It is an assertion of their import, a valuation that augments and interprets their happening. Can a professor's credibility be other than this filling in of import, the identification of values attaching to facts, people and events that deserve notice?

III

A professor's facility in his vocation obviously revolves around his capacity to show what is important to learning from the perspective of his discipline. He delivers believable answers to the "so, what?" question of students through the medium of his subject. When he is able to stir their interest in meaning and to show how that interest can be rewarded, he is bound to be believed. A professor's power to whet student appetites for meaning in their studies is the key to his credibility.

After visiting Dachau a few years ago, Viktor Frankl's work in therapy came alive for me. Frankl has made impressive the role of "the will-to-meaning" as the tap root of human personality. As a prisoner in Auschwitz and in Dachau, Frankl observed that the inmates died who ceased to search for some meaning in their brutal suffering and abandonment. Those who were, on the other hand, most able to survive were sustained by an unquenchable will to find some intelligible scheme in which their experiences fitted. His "logo-therapy" as a consequence of this experience in dealing with the alienation, frustration, anomie and psychotic conflicts of patients has attracted wide attention.[7]

Every student takes something to be important, his expected profession, social recognition, a personal life-style. In relying on this will-to-meaning the professor has the wind with him. It has the potential of bringing about recognition for the arrival of Godot. The teacher's task is to

---

[7] Cf. From Deathcamp to Existentialism (Tr. Lasch). Boston: Beacon Press, 1959, p. 49. Man's Search for Meaning (Tr. Lasch). Boston: Beacon Press, 1963.

9

show the import of learning in the context of values students already prize. Teaching successfully means showing that learning is not good enough until it stretches toward the fullest import available to man of any subject. What is presently taken to be important must be seen in relation to what else is important.

Such a conception of teaching amounts to saying that the will-to-meaning is more inclusive, ultimate, fundamental and reliable than Freud's will-to-pleasure, or Jung's and Nietzsche's will-to-power. Both perspectives on human nature have been profound analyses of motivation with enormous results. But both leave problematic residues of import for man and his society that educators must recognize and succeed in transcending.

What matters most to man, that is, bears the greatest import for him, is not merely what he wants. To shape learning as the "fulfillment of needs" easily becomes learning as fulfillment of human desires. Freud's delivery of these desires from repressions of conscience released them from some of the artificial inhibitions that do hamper growth. But such freedom for desires also repudiates much accumulated wisdom and experience of society. Attention to the import of desires shows them more often to be selfish, lacking in temporal perspective, dominated by the will-to-pleasure, rather than deserving unqualified expression. The American appetite for an ever rising standard of living and horror at the prospect of "reduced expectations" are too familiar to require comment.

Again, the most significant factor in motivation cannot be the pursuit of survival, the will-to-power despite all obstructions. A healthy personality is indeed an achieving one, with values made real and not merely envied. But the very distinction of man from his animal ancestors lies in his capacity for delay in responses. He considers remembered consequences of his and others' actions and brings to bear on his decision other goals, including self-sacrifice, more rewarding than those to result from immediate and personal domination. Nietzsche's effort at "transvaluation of all values" was the notorious model of the Nazi master race. It results in a ruthless individualism that undermines necessary civil collaboration and institutional action. It threatens civilization. A professor must be concerned with other and more reliable factors in motivation.

When the professor devotes his efforts toward arousing the will to find import in things and seeks to guide that motive, he comes to the next major question. He must make clear the most promising directions for these motives. A returned student drop-out, who had found drugs, hermit living in the woods, and direct self-instruction empty, put the problem to me succinctly. "When I was in school before," he said, "my courses seemed never to deserve my time. Now there are so many important things to master, I don't have time to grasp them for I don't know what comes first." He was bent on finding out "Who I am," but not sure where the most promising answers were to be found.

With such a student, the credible professor coaches him to search out what Descartes called the "unavoidable believables" in learning, the "can't helps" of Justice Holmes. The import of things, the values to be pursued, are not free-swinging entities to be appropriated like cherries from a tree or manna from heaven. "Good answers" are qualities of reference, lines of thought or action about which one feels sure of reward when pursued. They are determined by the character of objects, goals, images, principles which when entertained in the mind are somehow enriching. We take good men, good pictures, good ideas as unavoidably believable, not merely "the good" in general.

It is important to notice that the search in teaching for import extends to all phases of experience, our thoughts, feelings, imaginings, habits of worship, inclinations to play, disciplines of work. A credible professor searches for the

11

range of all values and not merely for those
that will point toward his view of moral conduct. Many have steered away from concern with
values in learning for fear it would give the
professor license to dictate morality. Such
dictation never was properly called "education,"
and restriction of value interest to morals has
been a crippling feature of value theory for
centuries.

If discovery of the import in any experience
means that some advantage is added to the inquir-
er, he is advanced thereby toward "the way it is,"
and learns more fully what he should pursue.
Reading The Forsyte Saga involves us in the complications of property. A value is a call for
implication or involvement, and a supply of some
context for a moment of experience. It is an attraction about an experience that makes us want it
prolonged or repeated, or somehow related to other
experiences. It is like a view from Pike's Peak
on a clear day. It invites us to remain there
and want to return.

A value or good, the import of something, is
the embodiment of a concept in its most ideal form.[8]
Like goods imported from a foreign country, a value
is an addition to the quality or condition of its
receiver. A "good" chair means all that one con-
ceivably could include in an object supplying most
adequately and irreducibly the function of a place
to sit. A "good theory" supplies most suitably
the theme for comprehending the data which it relates. Thus a botanist studying violets will always have in mind his concept of a "good violet."
A thing is what it is in its highest manifestation,
as Aristotle said. The plant in hand fits well or
ill the concept of the best violet the professor
can conceive. He "knows his violets" by reference
to the one he values highest, or bears the fullest
import for the concept "violet."

[8]Cf. Robert S. Hartman, "The Science of Value." In
Abraham H. Maslow, New Knowledge in Human Values.
New York: Harper & Brothers, 1956, pp. 20-25.

12

"Disvalue," "bad" over against "good," must imply in this context the absence of meaningful reference, the hindrance of comprehension, the disintegration of an ideal form. A "bad" theory is one that is confused and unsuited to the data it presumes to illuminate. "Bad" health is the frustration of ideal functioning in an organism. A "bad" professor would then be one who fails to show the import of events in experience, one who identifies facts without reference to the values, or ideal forms of which they are susceptible.

Valuation, i.e., dealing with the import of things, is no empirical science in the usual sense. But its validity stems from the relating of symbols and their capacity to make experience meaningful, in a comparable way to the function of symbols in "empirical science." A sense object weighed and measured in centimeters and grams can be verified by results of its use or disuse. A symbol is a way of "drawing together" (sym ballein) data of awareness for fuller comprehension of them. The symbols of valuation, for example, "well being," "adequacy," "harmony with things," "strength," "control of tension," all references to "good health," are so reliable as to serve as definite goals for nourishment, rest and exercise. To restrict the term "empirical" to sense experience is sheer dogmatism. Empiricism is the formulation of some features in experience into usable terms of reference, words, mathematical signs, images, that make the rest of experience intelligible and manageable. It includes values as well as facts, sense data as well as "impressions."

A common wall chart in many classrooms where chemistry is taught exhibits lists of elements and their valences. As nuclear reactions have become more familiar, charts showing the involvement of elements with each other are also in widespread use. Values do not have as sharply definable dimensions and as measurable reactions as chemical elements, of course. Nonetheless, they are the elemental factors with which learning is concerned. They invite guidance, and authenticate learning. A

13

table of them could as well adorn the walls of
every classroom to remind students of the components underlying and infusing the subject being
taught there.

Such tables of value vary here and there in
terms used, but the ultimate foundational concepts are unmistakable. Life or existence values, that underlie questions of disease and survival, suicide and growth, "reverence for life"
in Schweitzer's terms--are the base line for all
cultural efforts. Bodily values are good in
themselves as bouncing health and athletic excellence testify. Character, the form or pattern
of one's conduct that can be relied on, comprises
the structure of personality, the worth of being
a self. Economic values comprise the goods essential to family stability, educational pursuits,
friendship and social intercourse, enjoyment of
art and nature, cultivation of worship. Recrea-
tional values help to relieve the monotonies of
work, the stress of various endeavors, and to re-
build depleted energies. They are the more crucial as leisure mounts in the post-industrial
age. Sometimes work or vocational values need
to be listed as a specific category to emphasize
the potential of labor to generate independence,
responsibility and self-expression.

A wide range of social or affiliative values
thrive in the interrelation of persons giving
rise to growth, friendship, love and mutuality.
Sexual values, long considered secondary to social values, have in recent years become primary
in nearly every discussion of human relations.
Intellectual or truth values for many people are
only instrumental to "getting ahead," but they
offer their own reward to artists, cultural
leaders, and all who are concerned with the
uniqueness of human existence.

Aesthetic values dealing with the intrinsic
charm of sights, sounds, smells and other sen-
sory experiences enrich our contemplation of objects "good in themselves," glimpses of nature,
music and art we wish repeated. Ultimately for

14

most people religious values comprise their "peak experiences" in which their meaningful relation is apprehended to what stands beyond and yet within the passing flux of events.

Granted that experiences of these value categories vary widely, their fundamental centers of gravity are clearly identifiable. No pursuit of learning would be intelligible without implying some recognizable and communicable conception of how some, or many of them as the case may be, figure in the subject under discussion.

A credible professor may proceed to show that there are values in learning, some prior to others in the progress toward meaning in things, without fear of being charged a dreamer. In fact, the will-to-meaning cannot make headway without such value symbols. The fulfillment of concepts, the ultimate import of any symbol, must be kept in mind for all intelligible enterprises. Reward of the will-to-meaning proceeds by appropriation of symbols that refer both to tangible and to intangible features of experience, the seen and the unseen.

To say that the credible professor eats of forbidden fruit, who openly and consistently concerns himself with values in his discipline and their relation to all other values, is as misguided as the biblical literalist who says Adam and Eve were actually cursed by eating from the forbidden tree. Their will-to-meaning began that day. The fall of man was actually upward, as Hegel pointed out. Camus, in The Fall, leaves us staring at man's midpassage from savagery to civilization. Merely to acknowledge unrest of conscience, when neglecting to respond to the need for help by the woman who plunged into the Seine, as Camus's character does, only states the problem of human egoism. The credible professor will surely take into account such deepseated egoism in all men. His task is to search out its import, and help his students move the will-to-meaning toward some more intelligible perception.

15

There is no denying, nevertheless, the misgivings of those who try to keep the credible
professor out of the valuation business. Credibility easily slips into credulity or gullibility,
where values are concerned, the critics say. And
the professor surely must save his students from
this Scylla of romantic hope as well as the Charyb-
dis of despair.[9]

It will be argued by naturalists, for example,
that such a concern with values as the criterion
of scholarship presumes that a world of intangibles
is more reliable than tangibles. Whereas the affairs of the mind, such as imagination, feelings,
concepts, values, are in fact of a lower order of
being, and hence of trustworthiness, than the physical order of nature in which they occur. Fields
of force, patterns of measurable extension and temporal duration are the insuperable fundamentals from
which the "commands" or "determinates" of human action come, according to Henry Margenau.[10] These
natural events are indifferent to man's wishes and
thus his judgments of value.

Dr. Johnson's effort to refute by kicking the
stone Berkeley's view of mind as intrinsic to and
efficacious in managing nature was no more effective than this argument, however. If man's knowledge of any kind has reliability, it resides in
his capacity to interpret, revise, anticipate, as
well as remember his awareness of "what is there."
He does not remake the world in many respects according to his desires, but his valuation of his
relation to it is central to his very intelligence.
It is his "yearning for form," in Rollo May's terms,

---

[9] Henry Novotny, "Objectivity and Biased Skepticism
in Higher Education." In Sidney Hook et al., (Eds.)
The Ethics of Teaching and Scientific Research.
Buffalo: Prometheus Books, 1977, p. 62.

[10] "The Scientific Basis of Value Theory." In Abraham H. Maslow, op. cit., pp. 41-45.

which is prior to all other features of experience.[11]
This yearning, the tap root of valuation, makes logic
and science possible, by development of symbols which
organize experience.

An anxious, maladjusted person, let us remember, approaches a psychotic state when he gets "out-
of-touch" with reality. His valuation of things is
out of kilter. Symbols are disarranged and carry
wrong values. Acts of friendship may be taken as
tricks with dangerous motives. It follows that one
is "in touch" with reality as the signs of it are
adequately read and understood. Mental health,
intelligent functioning, in fact performance as a
human being, depends on a valid grasp of the intangibles, and not mere conformity to an "observ-
able" physical world.

Secondly, critics complain, such reliance on
valuations is risky because it elevates feelings
and intuitions above rationality. It is an appeal
to the abstract and the vague. One can get brain-
washed by evangelists for value like Suyung Moon,
the Korean, for example. Dionysius must be ruled
by Apollo, as the irrationality of Nietzsche and
fanatical racists demonstrate. Uncontrolled pas-
sion shown in numerous sex crimes destroys personal integrity and even human life. Pandora's
box would be opened by such appeals, it is argued.

Feelings of value, like the appeal of honesty,
it must be replied, are not unstructured, however
uneven they may appear, and dangerous when segre-
gated from each other. One "cannot feel differ-
ently" when a feeling of one kind mounts. Good
faith cannot be felt as cheating or wickedness
just, as deceit cannot be felt as honorable. So-
called ambivalence of feelings, when one feeling
is overlaid by another, as in "mixed feelings"
about draft evaders, does not deny the structural
character of an apprehension of good which each
feeling expresses.

---

[11] The Courage to Create. New York: W. W. Norton
Company (Bantam Books), 1975, pp. 149-50.

Along with separate feelings for value must be recognized the feel for wholeness, completion, or authenticity psychiatrists try to release in their patients. The "I" that Descartes made so central in all rational dealing with nature, man and God is a complex of hopes, fears, regrets, valuations of alternatives in thought and action. One "gets himself together" and "feels right" about his relation to the world when he senses that "I am being what I should be" in relation to "the-way-things-are."

Rationality is certainly crucial to responsible selfhood. But its materials, and the base on which a rational conclusion is finally acceptable, are composed of a feeling that it is "good," i.e., the best view that can be had. The obviousness of an axiom, the harmony of viewpoints, internal consistency of a theory, the warm glow of a "beautiful answer" to a problem, all are evidences of a present and dominating perception of completeness, a goodness that is ultimate and needs no further defense. Values have an authenticity of their own, but one not unavailable to reason.

Further, such a view of values in learning, the objector will say, results in privatistic judgment as the criterion of scholarship. Atomistic perceptions of truth, as well as other values, are the diabolic sources of hijackers, draft dodgers, individualistic interpretations of civil rights, that threaten the very life of democracy. It would give even more autonomy to artists whose supposed insights already show, it is alleged, that "there is no disputing about tastes." Scholars can't agree even when supposing truth to be "objective."

This subjectivity and separateness of values does make trouble when they are looked at in temporary, local, segmental terms. But the full import of nearly any subject or event has long range, wide-reaching references. It is the neglect of these larger references in valuation that creates intellectual and social chaos, not the limits of values themselves. Actually a gradation of import in values from the temporary and trivial to the purest and most universal can be seen when carefully examined. A Duke Ellington number can scarcely be said to have the universal magnitude of reference that a Brahms "Requiem" has. Kant emphasized the import of a falsehood by saying each action must be considered worthy of becoming a universal law. The social disaster of ignoring Kant's law of valuation is a standing warning against moral chaos.

Separateness in values declines also as their magnitude advances. They interpenetrate in their most authentic reaches. Jesus has been commonly regarded as a "beautiful" as well as "holy" character. The Pythagorean theorem is a "true" and "perfect" conception of what a right angled triangle must look like, just as Einstein's view of relativity was a "beautiful" insight into measuring behavior of physical objects. It would be hard to imagine a Bach festival giving rise to hard drinking, drug trips, and mob violence that have often attended the delirium of rock festivals. The beauty of Bach's music doesn't seem to "fit" such conduct. Music may be an invitation to foot-tapping at its most primitive level, yet to the most entrancing "trip" in imagination at its profounder levels. Aesthetic values at their deeper dimensions bear on other values too. "Beauty is truth, and truth is beauty" as Plato and Keats have said. The credible professor will not stop with concern for values at their most trivial level, except to show where the limits lie. Values belong to a detectable family of import or meaning that ramifies beyond first impressions.

Perhaps it is the danger of indoctrination that critics fear most when values in learning are emphasized. Scholarship, they say, thrives when it is free, atrophies when tied to values. Scholasticism inhibited natural science, as communism restricts inquiry into participational democracy and systems critical of dialectical materialism. Respect for the integrity of all

19

learners requires freedom for them to form their own values, it is asserted.

Dangers of indoctrination are easily overblown, I believe, though they are real. For I have always found it remarkably instructive that various forms of indoctrination are not only tolerated but encouraged outside the college campus. "Learning" fostered outside the classroom does take place in a great variety of settings, many of which are controlled and hence subject to "indoctrination."

Children "learn" much about conduct by indoctrination. There is a growing reaction against the trend of parents, for example, to "let the children decide" matters of moral value too soon. Preschool children have to be "given" standards of value before they are able to form them on their own. Capacity for valuation matures along with biological maturation. Lawrence Kohlberg distinguishes six stages from "preconventional" values of childhood to "postconventional" or self-chosen principles of objective validity in adulthood.[12] But no one moves automatically or unaided through these stages, as the increase in adolescent crime indicates. The "value vacuum" characterizing the life of many an adolescent results from abandonment in value guidance often under the guise of tolerance and desire for independence. Realization that assistance, if not indoctrination, is essential has been urged by Max Lerner. Its absence can "wreak almost as much havoc in the form of anomie as the absence of a loving adult. . .in earliest childhood."[13]

Does any one regret the aesthetic indoctrination of Mozart by his father, and the demand for perfect performance through his earlier years? A successful business formulates "company policy," which usually means the values in its product which are to be commended to the public, and the employment practices as well as production pro-

---

[12]"The Adolescent as a Philosopher." Daedalus, 100:4 (Fall, 1971), pp. 1051-1086.

[13]Op. cit., pp. 109-110.

cesses believed essential to a profit. "Briefing sessions" of workers are forms of indoctrination much beyond mere reporting of information.

Military branches of government hold clearly labeled "indoctrination schools." While more stress on civil rights and freedom of expression in recent years have encouraged many recruits to take such courses with tongue-in-cheek, the legitimacy of some "standards" (of value) is commonly recognized. Understanding and support of democratic values are expected of all governmental officers. Espousal of communism, or even refusal to support the U. S. Constitution, would result in the impeachment and dismissal of a senator, judge, or President.

Theologians point out that it has been the articulation and effective insistence on acceptance of doctrine by the faithful that has kept the churches alive across the centuries. Where members have been encouraged to be "free thinkers," vitality has sagged. A creedless church has soon disappeared. Such cultivation of faith extends to all age groups. St. Augustine's "I believe that I may understand" has been a cornerstone of Catholics and Protestants alike, despite the differences in creed.

Now every teacher has his doctrines. No one can deny his right, or even his necessity, to hold some values, such as the validity of democracy, the essentials of success, the nature of right or goodness. So too, his privilege to express such values belongs to his membership in a free democracy. The crux of the problem of indoctrination lies in the extent to which a professor may seek to "mould" the values of students. Tyranny over the minds of students by a professor's dictation of his own values when essential to passing a course would certainly be intolerable, and self-contradictory. For the professor's task is to assist the student's discovery of import in things, rather than continually to announce and retest his own discovery of values by seeing whether they are accepted by others.

Presentation of value options for a student's choice can scarcely be considered indoctrination, even though the penalty of a wrong choice may sometimes have to be enforced. If a student refuses to accept the value or import of Boyle's law for understanding the behavior of gases, he may have to be downgraded in a physics class, unless he can give reasons for its rejection. Where the alternatives are less sharply definable, as in sale of arms to developing nations, the sanctions are less certainly available. But the professor cannot avoid the duty to make clear what the options are and to enforce penalties for a student's ignorance of at least those pertinent to the course in which he is enrolled.

A credible professor cannot be charged with indoctrination so long as the center of gravity in his work is the commitment to values by the student, and not merely to those of the professor. There is a limitlessness in values, i.e., a reach of import beyond what has been apprehended at any given time, that should encourage the student and safeguard the professor against dogmatism, or finality in belief. His business is not to transmit fixed beliefs, or dogmas to students for them to memorize, but to show how his pursuit of values so far may aid them in finding their own.

Among the hundreds of professors with whom I have been privileged to work, the half dozen most outstanding, thus most credible in the estimate of their students, had some attributes in common. They were alike in strong-minded affirmation of what mattered most in their disciplines. They believed their discovery of import in features of their subject should be passed on with enthusiasm to students. But none of them expected students to imitate them by slavish adoption of their conclusions or life styles. They took pride in the "originality" of their students. In effect they agreed with Bronson Alcott's assertion that "The true teacher defends his pupils against his own personal influence."[14] But they

---

[14] Webster's Dictionary of Synonyms. Springfield, Mass.: Merriam Publishing Co., 1942, p. 728.

were emphatic in their insistence that their
students respond to the values, the import
their own studies pointed toward.

V

Credibility clearly must be distinguished
from popularity. Otherwise the good professor
would be authentically identifiable merely by
students' choice. Confusion on the campus and
discontent by the public with the accomplishments of academe discredit such a view of
credibility. There are some forms of alleged
credibility that must be false. Our concern
is with the professor who deserves to be believed, because he enables Godot to come.

If a professor, first of all, merely con-
firms values already held by students, such pre-
judicial teaching can scarcely be called teaching at all. Professors who advocated or assumed
white supremacy, especially in the South before
1954, had wide hearing. Some still do even in
the North, but the civil rights movement is
gradually overshadowing their influence. I can
still see the other-worldly glow on the apple-
cheeked face of many a fellow student at the
University of Berlin in 1931-32 when their Nordic
destiny was mentioned. But such teaching clearly
merged into "propagation" of a belief already
strongly held.

It may well be doubted whether Charles
Reich's The Greening of America would have become a best seller if it had not confirmed the
anxiety of youth "to be themselves" and to establish their own values as the foundation of a
new and vital culture. Reich's espousal of "Consciousness III," which presumably brings about a
new culture and puts an end to artificiality,
alienation, class hatred and shoddy work,[15] was
a call to noble aims. But it succeeded mostly

---

[15]The Greening of America. New York: Random
House (Bantam Books), 1972, pp. 9, 233.

23

in stating the problems our culture contains and asserting that youth would fix them. It reassured youth of their destiny with little help in realizing it.

Many values like courage, integrity, family loyalty, freedom in worship, deserve to be retained. But without their constant reexamination and testing by reference to changing conditions, the professor encourages dogmatism, not responsible pursuit of import in experience. Merely to confirm values already held may turn into prejudice formation, not teaching.

A second form of faulty credibility rests on affirmation of one value or scheme of values as superior to and definitive of all others. To deny some measure of autonomy and uniqueness to values wherever found may suffocate the very values taken to be prior. Galileo's persecution by the church reflected a restricted and static ecclesiastical conception of physical nature. Rejection of Darwinian evolution by many "Christian" colleges for so long testified to an honest dogmatism about biblical cosmology and anthropology that most scholars want to forget.

On a recent visit to Wilhelm Humboldt University in East Berlin, I had a long talk with a student in philosophy. He confirmed my fear that the base line of all subjects taught there was an explicit Marxian scheme of values. Each subject was pursued according to its consonance with that Weltanschauung. Talks with other students and some professors made this view of the university study clearly typical inside East Germany. Such a single economic base for learning predetermines the conclusions one will reach.

There is, on the other hand, a danger that the "openness" stressed in contemporary American culture will result in such tolerance of differences that anything goes. So far as this plurality of values calls for those that make their own way and bear an authenticity that

24

accepts challenges from all comers, it is a healthy sign. Those values which endure must nevertheless allow a range of vitality for other values too. A diversity of values, when given rein, allows them to test and refine each other. And this intercourse of values with each other is essential to responsible conduct. "Efficiency" as a value in productive work, for example, may well be challenged and reduced in validity when confronted by the values in health and growth of the productive worker. Profits of U. S. Steel have an accountability to conditions before the blast furnaces.

Rapid growth of "non-Western," as well as "black," "poverty," and "women's" studies mark a recognition that a stifling parochialism had characterized many cultural and humanistic courses up to the middle of this century. A professor inevitably brings to these new areas values with which he has been most familiar. His credibility test is whether he can undertake new perspectives without slavish loyalty to his old bench marks. A sentimental attachment to untried but sparkling and exotic new ones would be an equal mark of superficiality.

Church-related and independent but "Christian" colleges were founded to insure the central role of Christian values in thought and conduct. In addition to the grave economic problem of maintaining private educational institutions, secular values and the new, open and vital interest in non-Christian religions threaten the earlier eminence of these colleges. They can no longer expect the resources of sponsoring churches to assure their future. The pluralism of our present secular society demands that the Christian values fostered by such schools be able to win their way without political or economic favor. The acid test of these church-related schools lies in the infusion of vitality their scheme of values can offer to the secular values already found meaningful in their society.

Since I have spent most of my waking hours

as a student, professor, or administrator in one or another of these colleges or universities, their welfare has been of especial interest and concern to me. My reluctant conclusion about their waning influence stems from their frequent confusion of tolerance with indecision about the import of their own values. James Hitchcock has pointed out that "rising groups" do not apologize or temporize about their own values. A "declining group" is usually one that has begun to doubt the legitimacy of its own values at some profound level.[16] A diffident and overly tolerant willingness to allow Christian values to make their way, in "the free market of ideas" Justice Holmes termed the academic community, leaves their fate to the vector of forces created by secular advertising. It is possible to expound and defend Christian values, while inviting their competition with alternate perspectives, without dogmatism or a restrictive indoctrination.

Superficial if not spurious credibility, in the third place, may rest on the supposed autonomy of a discipline of study. Like cell growth in a cancerous organ, the curriculum in the typical academic institution tends to proliferate itself to death. A hundred years ago Oliver March taught at Northwestern eight subjects ranging from Greek through minerology to zoology. Now there are nearly that many subjects or divisions in the same department. The chemist approaches atomic and molecular relationships from an analytic, inorganic, organic, physical, physical organic, structural, high temperature, or some other viewpoint.

Sharpness of definition, accuracy in measurement, thoroughness of analysis, control of conditions and similar factors, are, of course, hallmarks of science, and they have had significant results. Our complex and technological age makes specialists necessary in nearly every profession or occupation. The crucial question

---

[16]"The Dynamics of Popular Intellectual Change." The American Scholar, 45:4 (Autumn, 1976), pp. 522-535.

is whether education can be content with specialization alone for any of its devotees. The confusion of aims and conflict of social pressures so widely lamented supply the answer.

Here again the basic issue for the professor seeking credibility is the point where his grasp on the import of his subject is "good enough." If he is content to have his knowledge confined to limited import, to have a few able to understand his views, to offer unqualified results that may be harmful to civilization in some contexts, such as atomic energy or food additives, he may not expect a widespread credibility. The unavoidable values in scholarship that bear some kinship to each other insist that the purely segmental scholar remain of limited reliability. The Toynbees in history, Whiteheads in philosophy, and Bronowskis in biology and anthropology have manifested painstaking accuracy of detail in their fields of study, but have also pushed on toward their ultimate import in the family of values.

What a specializing scholar leaves out may well affect or even determine the import of what is left in, as we noted above. Pasteur stumbled on the principle of immunization he had been leaving out when an assistant delayed injections of chickens with serum long enough to allow its organisms to incubate. A historian who "sticks to the facts," let us say of Lee's enforced surrender to Grant at Appomattox, might well ignore the bearing on its necessity of the economic superiority of the industrial North, the political sagacity of Lincoln, defection of escaped slaves from owners and Confederate forces, the destitution of southern whites following the Union invasions, prospect of further suffering and death of rebel soldiers, and so on. But most of us grew up on the supposition that it was Grant's superior generalship that defeated Lee, the southern gentleman.

Cries of disaffection by students are directed at their professors most commonly because they are left to "put it all together" on their own. Not understanding the full import of their professor's teaching, they are bound to wonder if there is any. The habits of thought which hinder so many faculty members from thinking in each other's terms, and their failure through inability or unwillingness to show the import of their subject to other disciplines, contribute to the low level of credibility assigned to many in the academic community. "Charles Beard," said Irwin Edman, who was one of Beard's students at Columbia, "made the questions of government the most vital that anyone could broach" because they "touched matters that lay far deeper than the forms of constitutional government."[17] Had there been more Charles Beards the turmoil of the '60s would have been much reduced and more nearly controllable.

Another limit to credibility must be confronted by the professor who promises to "educate" a student quickly. Neither the impact nor import of many actions are immediately detectable. Stress in learning on the concrete facts of a subject and how to use information for an immediate task are useful services, as in vocational courses like stenography, auto repairs, computer science, nursing, or salesmanship. Often it is the only learning some students have time or ability to master. Recent stress by the U. S. Department of Education on career education however, may easily confuse "education" with "training." "Unemployment" often means inflexibility or incapacity for adaptation to available jobs which has resulted from training instead of education. Such teaching is the work of technicians, not professors, or educators in the true sense.

Graduate and professional schools are continually beset by the threat that they will become "how-to-do-it" schools. Law schools content to turn out technicians, uninformed about the purposes of law and disinterested in the values destroyed by a guilty client, can only

---

[17]"Columbia Galaxy." In Houston Peterson (Ed.) Great Teachers. New Brunswick: Rutgers University Press, 1946, p. 188.

augment social instability. Physicians unqualified in perception of social problems of health
delivery, the values at stake in control of heredity, or the import of their patients' personal
problems, are not truly educated. The professor
contributing to such short range atomistic conceptions of professional education deserves but
limited credibility. Such vocationalism has import for wide ranges of value he neglects.

Fortunately, a movement toward stress on
human values in medical education has recently
been gaining momentum. For samples, the medical schools at Pennsylvania State, New York
State University at Stony Brook, and the University of Houston have been showing the way.
Such Institutes as Salk, at La Jolla, California, and the Hastings Center for Ethics and
Life Science at Hastings-on-Hudson, New York,
are making significant studies of the impact
which ethics, economics, social science and
biology all have for each other.

Humanities programs at engineering and
technological institutions, such as Massachusetts Institute of Technology and Lehigh University are manned by professors alert to the
danger of uncontrolled technology. Their presence in these universities, as in some others,
indicates official recognition of the role
values need to play in science. Yet the actual integration of the disciplines remains
a continuing problem. Engineering students
are so inclined to regard humanities as "something to get over with" as soon as possible.

Roscoe Pounds are still rare in law schools.
Such symposia as "Law and Human Values" recently
held by Louisiana State and Southern Universities are encouraging signs. Many law schools,
such as the one at Columbia University, offer
courses in law and social values. But the
legal profession largely remains devoted to
the defense of clients. Attorneys frequently
become political officers and community leaders.
Yet the profession can scarcely be considered

basically interested in prevention of crime
and the positive cultivation of respect for
law. Doctors' efforts to provide preventa-
tive aid against illness and to cultivate
public health are far in advance of the legal
profession in fostering the full impact of the
services they render.

VI

Credibility that transcends fads, fashions
of thought, short term results alone, and limited perspectives, while remaining free of pro-
paganda and indoctrination, must be the goal of
the responsible professor. As an inevitable
bearer of values, the credible professor becomes an adjudicator of the timely amid the
timeless.

Affluent America with its stress on freedom of thought and unrestricted action empha-
sizes immediate satisfactions. The lure of
distant values dims so often before the pleasures of consumption on credit. Yet order in
the teeming tumult of competing values will
not arise by some miracle of Providence. It
can come only from the rigorous venture an
aroused will-to-meaning can originate and sus-
tain. The credible professor will help to
establish this feature of his students' study
in a presiding role over their will-to-pleasure
and will-to-power.

Thomas Mann made much of "the pit" experience in his Joseph stories. The brazen and ar-
rogant Joseph was transformed into the resource-
ful and considerate counsellor of Pharaoh, able
to interpret dreams and provide grain to his
hungry brothers, through the experience in the
pit. His reassessment during hours of abandonment in the cave enabled him to take stock of
all that was happening to him and to trace out
the import of each experience. The credible
professor provides, in an important sense, a
pit experience for the refinement and redirec-
tion of the random, short-range, prejudiced
thoughts of his students.

Godot comes not merely by invitation, but by the orderly and persistent search of him, an indiscouragable pursuit of values. This search has the most chances of success when aided by a credible professor capable of showing the import or value of each factor in learning.

CHAPTER TWO

THE DECEIT OF DIOGENES AND
PRIDE OF PYGMALION

If the arrival of Godot is to be facilitated
by one who accepts the involvement of learning
with values, the professor's identity consists
in mastery of such implications. This century
is sometimes called "the century of the identity
crisis." What identity should be able to with-
stand the "trauma of self-doubt" a sober number
of professors have been experiencing?

Credibility requires the "fidelity in diversity" that Erikson finds crucial to identity.[1]
This fidelity is to values. The credible professor has found his way among competing and changing
interests to values that reliably represent the
import of affairs in his discipline.

Students are quick to detect the vague, shift-
ing, false, or inarticulate identity of a professor
when it appears. Those whose real interests are
only in research, or some commercial or political
involvement, or who teach for its prestige and
professional security bear "a great big H for hypo-
crite branded on their foreheads," says one student.[2]
They profess to be doing something their actions deny.
The "validity" of the professor's calling does perhaps require a reinvigoration of its "intellectual
and moral stamina" after the turmoil of the '60s.[3]

[1] Erik H. Erikson, The Challenge of Youth. New York:
Doubleday & Company, Inc. (Anchor Books), 1965, pp.
22-27. Cf. Robert Langham, The Mysteries of Identity. New York: Oxford University Press, 1977.

[2] Kate Haracz, "The Education of Kate Haracz." Change
(May-June, 1970), p. 12.

[3] Miro Todorovich, "By Way of History." In Sidney
Hook (Ed.), The Idea of a Modern University. Buf-
falo: Prometheus Books, 1974, p. xiv. Theodore
Gross, Dean of Humanities at City College of New
York, says that "open admissions" dictated such re-

That enlargement would apply unavoidably to the strength of the professor's unity-in-difference with respect to values. What values does the believable professor persistently pursue?

A credible professor devotes himself to the inalienable right of students to integrity, along with their rights to life, liberty and pursuit of happiness. This identity or integrity in person-hood refers to the articulation of values that organizes their experience and guides their pursuit of new knowledge. It results from their "lengthened critical attention span." A teacher's vocation calls for bravery to confront ambiguities and controversies that values in their elementary stages manifest.

The professor ventures, at least by implication, beyond the "doctrines of lines and figures" into the realm of "ambition, profit, and lust," by which Thomas Hobbes warned is the realm where doctrines are "perpetually disputed."[4] For if each professor's work concerns only the reduction of men's interests to their lowest common denominator amenable to scientific calculations, it abandons students at the point of greatest need. This is happening as vigorous efforts are being made to treat even the traditional humanities "scientifically." And further, the very reliability of the science employed may rest on some values open to question. Such a result can happen if values, inevitably entwined in science, are not carefully weighed.

I

Facility in finding the import or value of things will lead the credible professor to part company from those among his colleagues who retain, though frequently unrecognized, a deference

---

medial work as led many City College professors to believe they "no longer had a profession." "How to Kill a College." Saturday Review, 5:9 (Feb. 4, 1978), p. 19.

[4] Leviathan, I, II.

for Diogenes. Refusing to "get involved" with
marriage, property, political institutions,
ideals, or group interests of any kind, Diogenes
yet walked the streets of Corinth with a lantern
in search of any "worthy to be called a man," before repairing to his tub or "pitcher." Only
virtue or value in the abstract was his concern.

Professors as a class are concerned about
values of course. They differ in the degree and
frequency with which they believe their scholarship should be "involved." Diogenes represents
the classic deception that virtue is its own reward, or that it is even conceivable apart from
the import or reference of its proposed action.
For he asserted values in eschewing the involvement they inevitably require. He valued living
in a tub above residence in a decent house, and
dependence on the wealth begged rather than what
he could have earned.

Efforts at value-free scholarship are subject to the same deceptions. One conclusion
held over another is retained for its superior
value. Criticisms of Newtonian physics usually
rest on values or import found in quantum mechanics or relativity theory Newton was not aware
of. Criticisms of American democracy express, or
imply, a preference for Jeffersonian values not
longer evident, or Marxian principles deserving
recognition, or some other set of values taken
as bench marks. Either values are smuggled in
as some value authority, or else a kind of egocentric discontent with any contrary conclusion
remains the basis of decision in such "value-
free" efforts at learning.

American history has, to be sure, been
strongly influenced by prevailing sets of values
later revised or rejected. Colonial puritanism
made all value considerations subservient to religion and theology. Whigs and Jacksonians tended
to make moral decisions synonymous with political
objectives. The sectional interests of the North
and South dominated some school textbooks, and
male chauvinism has long been prominent in educa-

tion, political and industrial practices. But could scholars have functioned in a "value-vacuum" that value-free learning supposes to be possible? Would learning have had vitality and influence if it had had no reference to these sets of values? A value-vacuum is psychologically impossible, and practically useless because the most crucial ranges of learning and motives for its pursuit are held to be "worthy" of emphasis.

Reliable criteria of value are crucial, and they will be discussed below. A quick conversion to "life-adjustment," however, as a means of getting values back into learning would bring us little satisfaction. The credible professor guards his students against the myopia of their own experience, the bias of hasty conclusions, the limits of special interests and the chaos of atomistic and segmental learning. "Life-adjustment" may follow from such facility in valuation, but as an aim in teaching it remains vague and confusing. As well pursue "happiness" as an end in itself. The status of values can be as vague here as it is in Diogenes' ignoring of them.

Among his colleagues is another group from whom the credible professor needs to distinguish himself, namely the modern admirer of Pygmalion. Unable to find a woman acceptable to his standards, Pygmalion, it will be remembered, carved a statue embodying his ideals of womanhood and Venus granted his prayer to give it life. Recognizing the inevitability of indoctrination the professor of this outlook seeks to impart an ideal set of values to his students, hoping they will come to life in his proteges. A few colleges, such as Wheaton and Oral Roberts, still expect such a performance by their professors in inculcating Christian values. Some professors in many differing institutions gauge their success by the proselytes gained to their Richtung, or scholarly stance, be it behavior reinforcement, linguistic relativism, economic determinism, or psychohistory.

Values must indeed be "taught," or even forcibly induced, as stabilizers of conduct in children. Juvenals "must not touch" some things, be required to brush their teeth, eat spinach, and tell the truth. Values emphasized as absolutes and in isolation from each other, as in the Scout Code, may help to establish in early years their clarity, importance and durability.[5] Students beginning to study a new subject profit from a model, as a method in art or science, a usable criterion of truth in statistics, a goal in social planning.

It can even be argued that a professor is derelict, indeed immoral, not to set forth his Pygmalion-like ideals. Norms of value, whether in logic, morality, art, religion, or science, arise from group interaction and critical conflict of scholars, not from mere maturation of innate factors in conscience, intelligence or feeling. A student is entitled to know the professor's views accumulated from this scholarly world about the import of materials in his discipline. The student deserves to see what they may offer to him as a model or even starting point in valuation.

When value delineation and dictation become permanent devices for all stages of learning, however, they turn into "self-liquidating" ideals, as Daniel Boorstin would call them.[6] Such complete and continuing indoctrination involves the dissolution of the teaching ideal in the act of its fulfillment. By "giving" a student values he is led to remain "other-directed," lost in the struggle for his own self-directing identity. The father seeking by a visit to my office ways to get his son to "do better" in chemistry so he could get into medical school, instead of "wasting his time in music," illustrates the impossibility of such domination. That boy's identity was headed toward band directing, not medical service, and that's where he landed.

[5]Milton Rokeach, The Nature of Human Values. New York: Free Press, 1973, p. 5.

[6]Democracy and Its Discontents. New York: Random House, 1974, p. 86.

Supposing that values are completely "stable," that is, permanently fixed and communicable as perspectives on the import of things, as believers in Pygmalion do, is as fallacious as to hold that they are "unstable." Personalities grow and conditions change. Psychologists such as James, Freud, Jung and Erikson have stressed that values emerge and recede as the ego encounters conflicting perspectives. For a professor to convey a scheme of values in the expectation that the student should adopt them outright, ignores the dynamics of growth in the student's learning, as well as the ethical significance of his autonomy as a valuer in his own right.

Does this mean the credible professor's identity lies in his enthusiasm for _every_ value, wherever found, in the hope his students will find those suited to their taste and appropriate to their condition? Does he sing Whitman's "Song of the Open Road?"

> "You road I enter and look around. . .
> I believe that much unseen is also here.
> Here the profound lesson of reception. . .
> . . . .
> None but are accepted, none but shall be
>   dear to me."

Impatient of Diogenes' withdrawal from values, and wary of Pygmalion's too explicit effort to implant them, the Whitmanesque professor takes it as his mission to _expose_ students to as many values as possible.

Traditionally the humanities have been assigned this task of "heightening the sensibility" to values and their frustration in vicarious experiences afforded by literature.[7] Perspectives on heroism, pride, love, loneliness, cowardice, tragedy, confrontation of death, almost the whole gamut of values, can be gained in Shakespeare's

---

[7]Daniel Bell, The Reforming of General Education. New York: Columbia University, 1966, p. 176.

plays, or the novels of Dickens. Even the
decadence of the South as emphasized by Faulk-
ner and the he-man animal spirits of Hemingway
may be vehicles for identification and exposure
to values through foreshortened imaginative
experience.

Mathematics and science are sometimes taught
also as exposure to values, i.e., as humanistic
studies since they "help us understand ourselves
better as human beings." At St. John's College,
for example, Euclid's Elements are studied to
show how the human mind can function. It "re-
opens the question of human excellence," which
is the function of every "honest teacher," according to Robert Goldwin.[8]

As a leader of "Great Books" discussion
groups for a number of years, I took part in
the regular process of "reopening the question
of human excellence" both through literature
and science. I came to the conclusion that the
crux of such studies rests with "which values"
deserve election and cultivation. To nibble at
great values, that is, to be exposed to them,
without help in decision among them or digestion
of any can be and usually is an exercise in much
lost motion.

To be exposed to values is of course better
than to be left to ignore them. But for a professor to join students in the "common search"
for values, or merely to point toward those they
would otherwise miss, assumes students have an
equally reliable built-in capacity to determine
values and a will to embrace the most significant
ones. Or else it is implied that any values they
choose, so long as they are "committed" to them,
are legitimate.

It is "the aspiration for generality," the
genius of learning, that is slighted by the Whit-

_____
[8]"Teaching and the Shaping of Souls." In Sidney
Hook and Miro Todorovich (Eds.), op. cit., pp.
9, 40.

manesque professor. From private, single experiences one strives for a more clear and inclusive grasp of reality. One asks of each experience, "Is this it?" That is, does each experience fit a model, class, or generalization
that is good enough to rely on?[9] Progress in
learning occurs as the tension between the attraction of a given experience and its value
paradigm is satisfactorily handled. Integrity
of personality rests with skill in calculating
the conflicts of value interests, the confusions
of import in experience. Merely to expose a student to values begins the learning experience but
leaves it before its most crucial stages are
reached.

What education has to offer and should seek
to impart as "an intimate sense for. . .the beauty. . .and structure of ideas together with a
body of knowledge which has peculiar reference
to. . .the being possessing it," according to
Whitehead.[10] But this sense for the structural
import of things, the order of values significant
in learning, does not impart itself in the process of exposure alone. The segmental character
of nearly any college catalogue and the multiplicity of electives everywhere available testify to
this widely held fallacy. Students left to "put
it all together" are more and more seeking to escape from this freedom.

A laissez-faire attitude toward values by
professors surely has an inescapable part in the
confusion of values in this era. Jefferson's
assertion that "a ploughman" will decide a moral
issue better than a professor because he has "not
been led astray by artificial rules,"[11] assumes a

---

[9]Cf. Irwin C. Lieb, "The Image of Man in Medicine."
The Journal of Medicine and Philosophy, 1:2 (June,
1976), p. 163.

[10]The Aims of Education. New York: The New American Library (Mentor), 1955, p. 23.

[11]Letter to Peter Carr from Paris, 1787. In Phil-
lips Russell, Jefferson. New York: Dodd, Mead &
Company, 1956, p. 145.

moral sense that simply cannot be verified. A professor, whose recognition of value as the import of things in knowing and who considers this his peculiar vocation, can and should be the focal agent in his culture. He assists students in developing skill for detecting the import of events in experience that identify the tissue of reality. Learning means concentrating on what matters most in trying to get sense out of things.

II

A clear and reliable identity which makes a professor credible does not come to him by osmosis, or by chance, but from an explicit address and calculated concern with this role of values in learning. Yet, the typical professor gives scant attention to the formation of such identity.

At a recent retirement dinner for faculty in a prominent midwestern college, I asked a highly successful teacher what had impressed him most about the work of his profession during forty years' association with it. "The decline in professional standards of teachers," was his prompt reply. This observation was no lament for the good old days by a tired old man, but a considered judgment by one who had regularly studied the role of the teacher and carefully tested the results of his own work.

After interviewing hundreds of candidates for professorial positions over a period of nearly twenty-five years, I must record my dismay that relatively few of them had a clearly formulated conception of their aims as teachers. And practically none had a well thought out view of the role that values do and should play in learning. Most of them were planning to teach because they admired a graduate professor, "math came easily" for them, they "liked people," or believed the teacher was "important."

Credibility of many a professor is shaky because he has never worked his way through to an articulated notion that teaching ultimately concerns valuation. There is indubitable evidence that a sober number of them drift or back into the profession. This was Ruth Eckert's conclusion after studying seven hundred professors in thirty-two colleges and universities in Minnesota.[12] The typical professor serves in an institution similar to the one in which undergraduate studies were pursued. He begins his vocation five or ten years later on the average than the professional scientist or business executive. These factors indicate little expectation of such a career in undergraduate days, rather than one that is clearly formed about the needs and possible achievements of coming generations.

Some professors say it is "not uncommon" to formulate reasons for their choice of a profession after the service of teaching has actually begun. These reasons follow from an experienced congeniality with the task, rather than a plan for it. As one of them admits, this means a rationalization of what was really no decision.[13] "What circumstances made inevitable" frequently becomes the basis of decision. "We choose our careers. . .much as a stream of water selects its course. . . ,"[14] which sounds strangely like the valley of least resistance.

Often abnormal circumstances, such as the scarcity of professors during the "tidal wave" of students in the '60s, the illness of regular appointees, the accommodation of remote areas by "extension services," lead to invitations to

---

[12] *Job Motivations and Satisfactions of College Teachers*. Washington: Office of Education, Co-operative Research Monograph No. 7, 1961, pp. 80-82.

[13] Jay A. Young, "The Acceptance of Obscurity." In Robert O. Bowen (Ed.), *The New Professors*. New York: Holt, Rinehart & Winston, Inc., 1960, p. 73.

[14] Richard M. Emerson, "A Rational Idealism." In Richard O. Bowen, *Ibid.*, p. 115.

teach by "those who will do it." Recruiting of professors from other walks of life, moonlighting of all kinds, frequently results in time-serving rather than the comprehensive and articulate role of value leadership a professor should provide. Many appointees are "connected with education," rather than serving as cultural leaders with a clearly conceived professional identity. Whatever the reason for appointment, the value function of the professor deserves to be expected of him. But it is rarely the reason for appointment, it would appear.

Any dean will tell you that a vast majority of his professors consider themselves very good, that is, credible teachers.[15] Though a relative few have had explicit preparation in the craft of teaching, they as a class remain only mildly interested in explicit study of the problems in teaching. Kenneth Eble's recent canvass of many types of institutions in various parts of the country turned up extensive "respect" for teaching but little "enthusiasm" for putting it above other responsibilities of research and committee work.[16] Jerry Gaff, in a comparable study, found a similar attitude toward in-service programs to improve teaching on many campuses. They are characteristically considered an overload, usually funded by "soft money," i.e., temporary funds from sources outside the institution's budget, or otherwise "not in the main stream" of academic life.[17]

This casualness in choice of teaching as a profession, and the neglect of teaching as a craft by so many professors, account for the oft lamented absence of a coherent philosophy

---

[15]Cf. H. Taylor Morse, "Appraisal of the Educator." In Russell M. Cooper, Two Ends of the Log. Minneapolis: University of Minnesota Press, 1958, p. 181.

[16]Professors as Teachers. San Francisco: Jossey-Bass, Inc., Publishers, 1971, pp. 24-25, 27.

[17]Toward Faculty Renewal. San Francisco: Jossey-Bass, Inc., Publishers, 1976, pp. 176-181.

of learning in the typical academic institution. A diversified background can serve a professor well. But a clear notion of the basic values of learning does not arise automatically from the logic of a given discipline, or from all of them when associated in a curriculum. No subject "teaches itself" reliably. An academic institution in which such an assumption is widely held, and apparently this is the rule more than the exception, is bound to be a crossroads of confusing aims. It cannot be a community of knowledge.

A professor's truest identity consists in a persistent effort to find what it is good for man to become. Learning is valuable proportionate to its capacity in enabling the learner to excel what he has been. Its thrust is the exploration of possibilities that deserve to make up the unique future of each person. Knowledge of history, genetics, and the biological base of human action are, therefore, all preliminary to what a human being can become. The peculiar power of man is to deal with "what is out of sight," in Jacob Bronowski's terms.[18] Other animals are confined so much more completely to the ranges of present experience, the food, mate or danger immediately before them. Man is capable of "forethought," and that is the chief value learning makes possible.

So much of current education is backward or downward looking. Reduction of thinking to behavior, body language, glandular conditioning, transfiguration of complexes, or some other nonrational level, makes "actualization" of the human potential an incidental, if not miraculous result. It is coordination of reactions, supplement to splittings or broken connections in awareness, the pointing of facts toward values,

---

[18] The Identity of Man. Garden City, N. Y.: The Natural History Press, 1971, pp. 19, 14, 3. Cf. also George Deefer, "Science, Poetry and 'Human Specificity.' An Interview with J. Bronowski." The American Scholar, 43:3 (Summer, 1974), pp. 393-394, 403-404.

maneuverability in the presence of multiple environments, that learning should assist. Unless the professor can enable a student to rise to the "fecundity of knowledge" that Cardinal Newman spoke of, learning remains myopic and crippled. Knowledge should foster a growing propensity to increase meaningful, and therefore valuable, relations to other persons, nature, and ultimate being. Constant focus on man's physiological origins and present conditions leaves out the crucial question, "What next?" But answers to this latter question are the ultimate task of the professor.

III

If the professor's vocation is to facilitate the student's perceptions of value, that pursuit must be shown to be worthy of effort.

Students need, therefore, to be aroused first of all from their proclivity toward endless self-reflection. Reacting against the widely touted "depersonalizing" influence of technological society, that calls upon the individual to conform to the demands of nature, industry and institutional organizations, many students have retreated to their own reflections for inspiration. Release for impulse has become a strong demand,[19] along with search by transcendental meditation, sense deprivation, bio-feedback, drugs, or some other device, to find the hidden insights conventional study has not conveyed.[20] Preoccupation with "liberation," "rights," "ego strength," and concern with "subjectivity," the welfare of the inner life,[21] color much current scholarship.

---

[19] Mervin B. Freedman, The College Experience. San Francisco: Jossey-Bass, Inc., Publishers, 1967, p. 175

[20] Cf. Adam Smith, Powers of Mind. New York: Random House, 1975, Chaps. II and III.

[21] Robert Nisbet, Twilight of Authority. New York: Oxford University Press, 1975, p. 139.

45

No one can, of course, deny the value of introspection, the search for inner resources. But the professor must constantly stress the fact that selfhood is defined primarily by extra-spection. One must "find his place" before he can "find himself." Human identity arises in the performance of specific tasks, treatment of particular persons, the execution of choices in each hour, far more than by repeated hypotheses in fantasy about a possible self. Values that develop, stabilize, and enrich human life consist in the import of one's relations to a transubjective world.

This retreat to subjectivity presents a serious stumbling block to valid learning. By focusing prime attention on number one, it fosters self-interest, and "selfish education is no education," as Hardin Craig points out.[22] It leaves out rational reference to the world "out there" and heart-feelings for fellow beings. It is the relation of oneself to both these realms that requires most crucially a professor's assistance. Further, such supposed "learning" becomes a kind of magic, whereby a change in attitude or belief substitutes for a solution to problems. Rebellion against parental guidance, rejection of professional leadership, or indifference to institutional authority, may remove a student's sense of frustration. It does not contribute to his competence in dealing with the circumstances these representatives mirror,[23] which are the student's problems as well.

Mental health essential to reliable learning consists in a balance of experienced reality "out there" with imaginative spontaneity "in here." Learning that "this is the way things are" carries with it a sense of participating

---

[22]"Portrait: Hardin Craig." The American Scholar, 40:2 (Spring, 1971), p. 308.

[23]Cf. A. Van Dantzig, "The Dynamics of Adaptability and Adaption." In Paul Weiss (Ed.), Knowledge in Search of Understanding. Mount Kisco, N. Y.: Futura Publishing Company, Inc., 1976, p. 201.

in being as such, even when the discovery of "the way things are" is unwelcome. It may define our limitations, but it also generates a "love of one's fate," and a recognition of what one should be doing.[24] A professor may need to stir up the imagination of his students, but imagination can only be tested by the way its values root in the real world.

As a bearer of value the credible professor must, secondly, succeed in persuading students that pursuit of knowledge can yield import for a _real_ world. It is no mere "encounter with nothingness." The nihilism and skepticism of much recent thought, typified by the existential-ism of Sartre, and the antihistoricism of many a student, presumes that theoretical "knowledge" is futile. Only present action yields a reliable basis for decision. Theory will in all probability, it is believed, yield indoctrination by a faulty past. Experts disagree anyway, and textbooks are dry and impractical to hordes of students.

Shock at the suicide of a student part way through one of my courses in philosophy impressed me indelibly with the urgency for a professor to make clear the possibility of _real_ meaning in knowledge. A professor may, when recognizing this obligation, point to the imperious demands of nature made by rules of good health, the in-exorable influence of other people, the irrever-sibility of time in the movement of physical bodies, the fact that "My heart (as well as Words-worth's) leaps up," and is not cast down, "when I behold a rainbow in the sky." Further, he must bear testimony to a texture or knowable tissue in physical nature and biological organisms, such as can be found in the fact that bees and ants com-plete but part of cycles in the activity of their hives or hills, which their lifespan cannot encom-pass. Such systems cannot be accidental or knowl-edge of it unreliable.

---

[24]Cf. Rollo May, _The Courage to Create_. New York: W. W. Norton Company, Inc. (Bantam Books), 1975, pp. 141, 148.

Approximate answers to questions, of course, even when based on extensive evidence, and held with due care for bias and partiality, may be the best we can do with some subjects. Even a doctor's prescription is based on probable reactions. But that does not make knowledge futile, or approximation wholly erroneous. The accomplishments of modern science, whatever their threats and residual problems, are too well established to make nihilism sensible.

Unless "bonum et ens convertuntur," value and being of things are interchangeable and inherently related, no conclusions about anything could be reached, even that skepticism is necessary. To make action superior to theory is to remove the very barriers to mindlessness and superficiality the "practical" man abhors.[25] Efforts at therapy currently so popular would all be undercut if patients could not be related to an _understandable_ world. Who is prepared to admit that _all_ dialogue is with nothingness? Insanity would be the only fate if efforts at knowledge had no landmarks reliably identifiable.

A third hurdle the professor seeking credibility must pass over is this inevitable relativity and partiality of some knowledge. Acceptance of relativity to time and place as a crucial footnote to all physical measurements has common recognition. The increased world contact through travel, cultural exchanges, news reports and industrial operations has brought to everyman new knowledge of competing lifestyles and ideals, cultural traditions and values.

"Freedom," "success," "holiness," "culture," "art," and similar values certainly do not mean the same thing to a Russian, Chinese, Indonesian, Ugandan, or Egyptian as to the typical American. Indeed Americans vociferously disagree among themselves on many occasions as to the "objectivity"

---

[25] Francis Canavan, "The Problem of Indoctrination." In Sidney Hook (Ed.), _The Ethics of Teaching and Scientific Research_. Buffalo: Prometheus Books, 1977, pp. 30-31.

and reliability of judgments about such values.

Deduction that values are subjective and only "relative to the situation" regularly confronts the professor. In Bethesda, Maryland, a high school principal was recently convicted of shoplifting, but defended by hundreds of students because he was "a good principal." A well-known Washington columnist has supported the Director of the Office of Human Rights in the District of Columbia for submission of work done by subordinates but represented as his own to qualify for a Ph.D. degree. These thieves were taken to be "good men when viewed in the right light."

Flexibility in judgment to accommodate new and complex circumstances deserves much of the emphasis Joseph Fletcher has urged.[26] But "good" can only be a valid assertion when the judgment has criteria that rest on more than private feelings, and conditions of the moment. It "diminishes our dignity as human persons" if we try to "escape the burden of decisions in the relativities of our human situation," in Tillich's terms.[27] The world has condemned Richard Nixon for his failure to recognize the imperatives of the constitution, the requirements of truth-telling despite the circumstances during the Watergate scandal and since. Generality, or objectivity of judgment has been supposed possible in estimating Watergate conduct.

"Truth" is to be sure a firm grip on some part of reality. Its validity may stand, however, even when qualified by its grasp in some other time, or by some other person. Otherwise pursuit of knowledge, or of any other value, is vain and contradictory. Max Planck, tormented by the Nazis, saw the need for some over-arching metaphysics or theology to give objectivity and perspective to the partial views of truth his science set forth. The political claims of expediency defended by Hitler did not allow standing to legitimate truth, he be-

---

[26]Situation Ethics. Philadelphia: Westminster Press, 1966.

[27]My Search for Absolutes. New York: Simon and Schuster, 1967, p. 101.

lieved, though statements of it must be partial.[28] Part of the truth cannot serve for the whole, nor one value stand for others. Apprehensions of value are private and variable transactions, but the values to be grasped are "there." Otherwise "good" is a meaningless assertion.

It follows that a fourth service the student needs in perception of value is some inclusive perspective within which the discipline he studies represents a fragment.

The "holiness of depth" since Sputnik has become synonymous with "excellence" to many, perhaps the majority of professors. Broad amateur development through education has been replaced quite generally by the specialized expert as the complexity of an urbanized and technological society has advanced. As a consequence, a few values are sought in learning by each professor to the neglect of others. The professor comes to fear he cannot operate with confidence in a context beyond his limited specialty. A nineteenth century English literature specialist may be considered a "good authority" though he knows little of biological science. It would belittle the importance of literature to try to master science too!

Typically each discipline stipulates its own problems and values, specifies its own concepts and techniques. Society is less and less able to shape learning to its own broad aims. The onrush of minorities to gain attention to "their values" has usually resulted in some program of "special studies." The "service" of the academic community most often is regarded by the public and a growing number of faculty members as the supply of expertise to a specific problem identifiable within the range of some division's special interests.

It is primarily the student hatred of this segmentalism in academe that has generated their

---

[28] Cf. George N. Shuster, Education and Moral Wisdom. New York: Harper and Brothers, 1960, p. 123.

demand for "relevance." Brushed aside as superficial and immature by some professors, this sum-
mons for a higher level of generalization to embrace their bits and pieces of "knowledge" deserves,
however, a more thoughtful and reliable response.
Without some inclusive scheme of meaning the values
in any study frazzle out and lose their identity.

Obviously specialized scholarship has im-
proved the quality and accuracy of matter taught,
made better methods of teaching possible, weeded
out the careless student by its exacting demands,
and helped to meet the needs of a specialized society. The limits of specialization have also
been pointed out. It generates the "anti-leader-
ship vaccine" John Gardner warns of, for a leader
is no specialized technician, but one able to "put
it all together." The reverberations of specialized studies can be dangerous, as the possibility
has arisen of creating uncontrollable organic monsters by rearranging DNA balances in genetic experiments. Unemployment has become a serious
national issue in this country, and in parts of
Europe, because knowledge is segmental and skill
in work constricted to a narrow range.

A credible professor cannot shrug off the
problem of breadth and depth even in a professional school. His task is one of "expanding
relevance," in which the learner's intelligent
relation to his entire environment is shown to
the degree time allows. Growth in learning
does not mean effectual development of every
possible relation, but the perfecting of those
that contribute to human welfare and uniqueness.
Overgrowth of cells is a condition of cancer, as
overgrowth of an unrelated segment of knowledge
signifies confused meaning or illness of truth.

Every professor can be expected to locate
his studies in some higher levels of generalization. He needs to set forth a broader range of
values that justifies concern for those he wishes
to stress. Thus, genetics concerns the values of
knowing relations among the generations of organisms. But these are of importance to the extent

51

that the total health of that organism may be affected. In the human organism, these physiological values obviously impinge on the psychological values, and in turn on sociological, ethical and cosmic values.

Conflicts within and between these levels of value can be transcended as a "higher" perspective in each instance is reached. Functionally different values have their legitimate range. The task of the learner is to reach such a point of elevation in his perspective as to grasp the relation of mountains and valleys, rivers and meadows, lions and lambs as part of the same landscape.[29]

The supposed conflict between vocationalism and liberal arts can be reduced from "difference" to "differentiation" in purpose. The values in diverse kinds of learning can be related by a credible professor. The more mature and insightful the professor the better this correlation and comprehension can be fostered. Edmund Pellegrino's suggestion as a doctor that physicians as well as all specialists should have "a philosophic sense," is a good one,[30] and notable as coming from a non-professional philosopher.

A professor capable of assisting students to grasp the values or import of their subjects is no mere "see and tell" narrator of facts. He cannot leave his subject for students merely to sample or neglect. He may not leave fragments of information untied to their valuational context. Nor can his loyalties lie only with the new dimensions of his discipline, important as they are. No longer expected to save souls, the professor has the obligation to save minds, as Commager puts it. It is the salvation of students from value-disorientation that is the focus of the professor's identity.

---

[29] Oscar Van Leer, "To Widen Horizons. A Task for Education." In Paul W. Weiss, op. cit., pp. 231, 236, 227.

[30] "Philosophy of Medicine: Problematic and Potential." The Journal of Medicine and Philosophy, 1:1 (March, 1976), p. 26.

His task is to persuade students, not as a politician or salesman persuades a customer with biased appeal to support a program or buy a product. But he is to make plain by rational means, open to all criticism, that the values that matter are the common possession of mankind. He urges the intrinsic value of objective inquiry transcending self-interest. He dares to assert that such pursuit of knowledge is rewarding and not vitiated by the relativities of time and place. And he sets that search in a context of more and more inclusive perspectives, not in the belief that each is "final," but that it is the scaffolding by means of which a still more reliable insight can be profitably pursued.

IV

What this discussion about a professor's identity comes down to is that scholarship needs a face-lifting. The supposition which has gained such momentum in the last two centuries that fact and value are two separate features of "knowledge" has shown its unmistakable limits. Specialization in scholarship has come full circle to repudiate its own reliability. The accuracy and thoroughness of specialization must not be given up, but supplemented by valuational interconnections.

Value is not merely a means of weighing facts when found. It is intrinsic to the very identification of fact. The particular "facts" of this maple tree are not static observations. They are in process of flourishing as an illustration of "maple," or declining and fading from such differentiation. They represent a healthy or decaying tree, just as human skin is "healthy" or "diseased" to the doctor, or the state is a more or less democratic or fascist state to a politician. They give rise to a good or satisfactory grasp of "maple tree" according as they mesh in the best notion of "tree" we can muster.

It is instructive to note that the term "value" is derived from the Greek word "arete,"

which meant "virtue," "good," or "healthy."
Plato and Aristotle thought of excellence in
bodily health as "arete." Observation of what
a thing "is" cannot be separated in Greek, as
in any language, from what it is tending to become, and thus by reference to what it should
at its best become.[31]

Further, facts that are "objective,"
"scientific," or "legitimate" are so identified
by virtue of the import or value they manifest.
"True" or "pertinent" facts about saccharine as
a possible producer of cancer are held to be so
because they line up in a generalization about
their harmful results on bodily tissue. Thus,
values claim rootage in "the way things are"
as unavoidably as facts. They require cognitive
recognition as fully as facts.

It is wholly arbitrary to maintain that the
scholar comes to his work free of value assumptions, willing to deal only in fact. He brings
with him some conception of what the truth is he
has so far found, and how one ought to live as a
consequence of his best thought up to that time.
These assumptions are the very tools of his
study. In other words, the reliable, credible,
scholar faces the role of value in his thought
and explicitly addresses himself to the way he
and his students may most reliably deal with
these values. Values are a fact, as surely as
facts have value.

Rather than discourage the professor with
the threat of subjectivity such a recognition
of value might induce, it should shift the focus
of much of his work. He has run the risk of arbitrary valuation all the time. His only choice
is to identify, clarify and systematize the value
factors in his discipline if he would become a
reliable scholar. If he seeks to become a credible

---

[31]Cf. Martin Diamond's "Teaching and Politics as
Vocation." In Sidney Hook and Miro Todorovich,
The Ethics of Teaching and Research, op. cit.,
1977, p. 18.

professor he will cultivate skill in enabling
these values to impress his students with their
freight of meaning.

Plato seeking to find the relation of all
ideas to "the good" would be a better model for
the professor than Diogenes, Pygmalion or Whitman. Is it not the value of any idea that makes
it worthy of a professor's time, or the effort
of instructing students?

V

No conception of a professor's identity could
be reliable when merely viewed in the abstract
and divorced from the condition of student clients
for his work. The value-filters each student
brings to college condition what a professor can
be expected to accomplish.

Classification of students according to these
filters varies widely depending on its purpose.
From reading Charles Reich's The Greening of America
and Theodore Roszak's The Counter Culture we are
left with the impression that a provocative new
consciousness of direction has arisen among students. It is implied that professors must not
only reckon with it, but define their identity
thereby. Yet what sectors among students call
for which responses, and how their values are to
be tested remains ambiguous. The Scranton Report,
on the other hand, concluded that students as a
group were not seriously discontent with higher
education as such, but mostly with campus regulations.

A more careful delineation of student groups
was offered in the Fortune article, "What They
Believe."[32]   Twenty per cent of the students considered were found to be "forerunners" seeking to
explore the world, and concerned with their own
identity. By implication they were dissatisfied
with higher education. Yet, as pointed out by
Eble, there is no one set of things all students

_____

[32]79:1 (Jan., 1969), pp. 70-71, 179-181.

want, or are capable of. Even the typical human wants of love, respect, security, freedom have different degrees of value for different students.[33] So far as generalization is permissible, a characteristic concern can be noted for larger communal or brotherly opportunities for the oppressed, and less restraint for all on individual life-styles. Above all, students quite commonly come to college wanting professors to <u>care</u> about their values.

Recognizing that the size of membership in groups varies from campus to campus, the professor can usually count on three categories of filters to the value process with which he needs to be occupied. It is his obligation on a given campus to assess as carefully as possible the proportion of students in each category. The professor's strategy in value cultivation, and hence his vocation, will be colored by the distribution of students to be instructed.

Some proportion of students, perhaps a fourth on many campuses, are authoritarian personalities beyond the usual uncertainties of freshman beginnings in college. They continue to be wary of inexact answers to their questions, distrusting intangible values, speculative thought, "creative" and unconventional methods of instruction. The influence of parents continues basic in vocational plans. Their moral standards are less likely to be rigid, but the values of early peers, church and home remain much in the form they were before college. They are inclined to judge the adequacy of college study by its support of early value standards and confirmation of pre-college expectations.

It is easy for a professor to feed his own ego by supposing that such students need above all to be shocked awake by him, to "get them to thinking," and to break up caked habits of childhood. Belief in the importance of such aggression can obscure the positive role of established values every professor needs to recognize. Each student has a right to the continuity and stability

---

[33]Op. cit., p. 76.

such tenacity represents. So far as successful teaching involves respect for students and acceptance of "where they are" as a beginning for instruction, the professor must work with these values patiently.

Many of such traditional values are contradictory of course, as for example, belief in instant pleasures of credit buying and the satisfactions of rigorous thought, which are only possible after long discipline. Some early certainties are sheer prejudice. Demonstrations at Columbia University against appointment of Henry Kissinger, as a professor after his service as Secretary of State and his involvement in Vietnam, revealed student prejudgment that he could not be impartial about political issues.

Emphasis on research and cultural criticism, common stock-in-trade of academe, when added to fears of indoctrination, however, often leave the professor in a negative stance toward established student values. Let him remember, however, that in the investigation of his own discipline, the professor habitually hangs on to the certainties of fact, principle and method while he explores the uncertainties. A student is entitled to the same treatment respecting values. His tolerance of uncertainties can be fostered best while he harbors his certainties. If the net effect of a professor's teaching is wholly negative, in the sense that it shows students what values not to hold, such teaching is only half-way successful. Negations of value involve affirmation of alternative values. But if these implied values are not articulated, teaching denies its profession.

Another group of students, sometimes not more than five per cent of the total, come to college as articulated radicals, the bright iconoclastic critics of the establishment. They were the noisy leaders of the unrest in the '60s, but they are yeast in most every student generation. Usually of higher intelligence than the campus average, these students, often

from broken, but certainly from unconventional
homes, have high self-confidence. The authority
of their own convictions usually challenges institutional regulations, curricular plans, and
traditional instruction. They disdain the
desiccated intellectualism of many "established"
scholars and demand that the campus note with
care "how we feel" about things.

Unresourceful educators are inclined to regard such students as "the enemy," rather than
vessels of special opportunity in value cultivation, which they really are. Their fresh approach to learning and bare-handed demands for
its results have shaken up many a campus deadened
by rigidity of outlook.

Some of these students are ready for "the
leap toward the marvelous" Saul Bellow takes to
be vital to a lively culture. Their demand for
joy in learning is wholesome, since its effect
on the enlargement of life should indeed be ex-
hilarating. Some of their values have given
new impetus to civil rights, etched more fully
the evils of war, especially in Vietnam, and
made more hollow the materialism of a consumer
civilization. A professor usually finds these
students ready to take values seriously.

Yet, the credible professor has significant
revisions in their outlook to bring about. Their
zest for first-hand experience typically depre-
ciates vicarious learning, without which even
the reading of a book would be a waste of time.
Arrogance in judgment of their elders, the events
of history, the contributions of institutions,
often distorts their valuations. An exaggerated
validity assigned to feeling may becloud rational
and critical judgments. Sometimes the resistance
to competition, as in the down-play of grades and
honor societies, really masks undisciplined lazi-
ness. These unbroken colts can be taught to run
fast, nevertheless, and the alert professor
sees the makings of value in their antics.

No doubt the majority of students on nearly

every campus can be considered rational, open to instruction and value guidance. Value formation for the common run of students is not fixed and predetermined by their early setting. Nor are typical students so obstreperous in their reactions to established values as to waste the time of a professor in convincing them that wisdom has not waited for their arrival to have its day. They can be persuaded.

The three best teachers I had in this country and in Germany were alike in their expectation that I would stretch to the limit of my abilities. One taught Latin in high school, another educational psychology in college and the third philosophy in graduate school. Without saying so the three conveyed to me that mere casual knowledge of their subjects was unforgivable. I was lured toward the ideal implications of every term, thought and principle. The expectation that I would reach for the full value in every effort at learning was an irresistible invitation to the excitement of learning that to me has never dimmed.

Values have faded from much teaching through a take-it-or-leave-it attitude of professors. Not enough is expected of students. The desire for objectivity by professors has meant to many students that their responses don't really matter. Instruction in large groups so easily reduces teaching to the conveyance of information to a passive crowd unable even to get in for office hour conferences. Grading by a teaching assistant removes the possibility from a professor to decide whether his expectations are met, except in a stylized set of answers the assistant uses as a guide.

Instruction in such masses as are found in the large majority of campuses means that the American pattern of higher education leaves out the expectation of value formation in any serious way. For to do such instructing the professor must be able to hold up expectation of value pursuits, and be able to see whether there is any

59

adequate reponse. In the tennis game of teaching, the student's return is fully as important as the serve into the proper court beyond the net. The identity of professors will not include value development of students if they are not within range of such direction and return for their efforts. Sufficient responsiveness of students is available on every campus. The value neutrality and practical neglect of students because of numbers often stand in the way of the true value identity every professor should seek. This is especially true of some of our largest learning centers.

In smaller institutions where value cultivation is more possible, many professors have become indefinite in exercise of this possibility. With decline of church-relatedness and the appreciation of sectarian values has come a neutrality about many other values. "Christian values" have been many times more formally saluted than explicitly affirmed. The tendency to ape the university and professional school, "so the majors will get in," is a relentless foe of articulate and persistent attention to values as such, and to their diverse ranges.

It is hard to deny Eddy's conclusion that, "The contribution of the college is to force values into consciousness," that is, to recognize their inevitability, "where they may be reexamined and refined."[34] It is this vocation of the professor that must be reappraised. Its centrality as the ultimate identity of the teacher calls for a new focus by professors, administrators and by parents as well as the supporting public who have felt their hopes of higher education were not being fulfilled.

---

[34]Edward D. Eddy, Jr., The College Influence on Student Character. Washington: American Council on Education, 1959, p. 174. Martin Buber recognizes that an "infinity" of form-giving forces play on students. But it is the conscious selection of what is to be taken as knowledge and stipulation of what "should be" which is the "fundamental vocation" of the educator. Between Man and Man. Boston: Beacon Press, 1955, p. 106.

CHAPTER THREE

HEARTBREAK HOUSE OF INTELLECT

I

Important conclusions follow concerning the academic community, if a credible professor's commission does not allow him to ignore or seek to detach his teaching from values. A "house of intellect" that resists all anti-intellectual distractions, such as Jacques Barzun urged in his volume by that title, would be one in which rational and orderly pursuit after the value import in things was clearly its purpose and the consequent propagation of such values its practice. Professors in such an institution would take such concern with value as their vocation. But such efforts are not the thrust of the typical professor, nor longer the expectation of the average academic institution.

Morris Freedman's indictment of higher education as an enterprise not knowing where it is going, or where it wants to go, ". . .all the while. . . proposing new ways of getting somewhere,"[1] was so severe as to be ignored by most practitioners. Nevertheless, the congeries of unassimilated purposes the institutions of learning not only tolerate but often encourage today, leave about the only common denominator of learning to be the hope that it will somehow help students make a living. If this is the only true value sought in learning, education is shortsighted, materialistic and ultimately self-defeating. It is contradictory to presume that pursuit of "truth" is education's purpose and act as if only vocational "truths" matter.

This malaise infects both public and private institutions. With the loosening, if not dissolution, of church-relatedness on the part of many liberal arts colleges, together with their stress on the specialization and vocationalism many believe necessary for survival, such explicit value

---

[1] _Chaos in Our Colleges._ New York: McKay Company, Inc., 1963, p. 9.

cultivation as these institutions once sought has dimmed. The legal mandate of public institutions to be neutral on religious and political issues, in addition to the widely held professorial convention that true scholarship is value-free, has led to their conclusion that value cultivation is both impossible and unwise. Credibility that rests on what a professor does with values, as outlined in earlier chapters, has in most academic institutions a barren soil in which to take root. Academe has indeed lost control of its destiny if its purpose is to find "knowledge" without some integrating principles of valuation.

George Bernard Shaw's characterization of culture in England before World War I as "heart-break house," called attention with chilling vividness to the economic and political confusion through neglect that had generated a moral vacuum. With interest by the influential in politics at a low ebb, England delivered itself over to "ignorant and soulless cunning" with frightful consequences, according to Shaw. Disdain for all utopias was nevertheless accompanied by hypochondria and superstition. ". . .Soothsayers, astrologers and unregistered therapeutic specialists" flourished in the previous half century as never before in history. Captain Shotover's efforts to explode dynamite by mental force and to attain "the seventh degree of concentration" in perfect tranquility[2] would not sound strange on many a college or university campus today. American houses of intellect invite such confusion by their neglect of explicit exploration and rational cultivation of values implicit in learning. They now spring up where they will.

II

Recent studies of value in learning do not offer much guidance to the professor's ideal of credibility. The status of values resulting from instruction, according to traditional standards of scholar-

---

[2]Introduction to Heartbreak House. Six Plays by Bernard Shaw. Dodd Mead & Company, 1941, pp. 450-455, 492.

ship at least, is subject to widely varying interpretations.

Philip Jacob's well-known study touched off
in 1957 a wide-ranging discussion of values that
still goes on without uniform conclusions. His
observation, that the values of college graduates,
which could be expected to distinguish them from
non-college persons, are actually little different,[3]
would mean basically that students learn very little
of importance from formal college instruction.
This conclusion follows from the view of learning
emphasized here that learning involves an ideal
import or "best" value in concepts employed.

Findings by Feldman and Newcomb[4] point essentially to the same conclusion that values of students do not change significantly regardless of
the method or quality of instruction, or the curricular pattern, including courses in social science. More recent studies by Gerry Gaff and Alexander Astin[5] echo the same conviction that values
change notably only in the small college, and
single department or college in a university,
where contact with students is frequent outside
of class, and convictions about value are shared
in unhurried personal communications. Barriers
to such contact are, however, significant on most
campuses. Age, cultural development, busy sched-
ules, research aims of professors, location of
their offices, and the number of students most
professors must teach, restrict these possibilities
to a minimum.

Critics of Jacob, such as Allen Barton and Paul

[3]Philip Jacob, Changing Values in College. New York:
Harper & Brothers, 1957, pp. 50, 8-9, 5.

[4]K. A. Feldman and T. M. Newcomb, The Impact of College on Students. San Francisco: Jossey-Bass,
Publishers, 1969.

[5]Gerry Gaff, et. al., College Professors and Their
Impact on Students. New York: Wiley & Company, 1975.
Alexander W. Astin, Four Critical Years. San Fran-
cisco: Jossey-Bass, Publishers, 1977, pp. 50, 230.

Lazarsfeld, declared that the design and methods of his study were unreliable and that his conclusions could be taken only as "challenging hypotheses."[6] Keniston and Gerzon have contended that such extant studies do not hinder their own conclusion that attending college has undeniable "major effects" on students beyond the information acquired and skills attained. College study has a "liberalizing effect" which increases "open-mindedness," "a perspectival view of truth," "individuation of moral judgments," and "psychological autonomy." It decreases, they contend, "dogmatism," "intolerance," "conformity," and "dependence."[7]

Whatever the studies show about the value process, significant changes in student values have occurred since World War II that scarcely require enumeration. The "counter culture," emerging from disillusionment with mechanized production as well as consumption, and constrictions of powerful institutions, has remarkably widespread support.

Acceptance of many established institutions has clearly eroded, institutions long considered essential to a stable society. Not only has the authority of parents declined in the choice by their children of friends, recreation, social life, vocation and place of residence, but the importance of marriage itself is increasingly doubted. Efforts by parents to give children "better opportunities" have often led to divorce by the latter of the "new life" from its progenitors. "Alma mater" has been stripped of much sentiment, its program and officers considered wise only if proved by results. Some students take education to be a legal guarantee of "success." A recent court decision was necessary to save the University of Bridgeport from payment of damages to a student unable to get a job upon

---

[6]Studying the Effects of College Education. New Haven: The Edward W. Hazen Foundation, 1959, p. 76.

[7]Kenneth Keniston and Mark Gerzon, "Human and Social Benefits." In Background Papers, Universal Higher Education. Washington: American Council on Education, 1971, p. 54.

graduation.[8]

Government manifestly has also suffered a notorious credibility gap since the secret operations attending the Vietnam War and Watergate have come to light. Military service is no longer considered the patriotic duty it was in World War II but may be "dodged" and amnesty expected. Wars are not considered one-sided issues, and their devastation is declared unjustifiable under nearly any circumstances. A student demonstration is still probable when war most anywhere in the world threatens.

Belief in individual rights has become a powerful force. The ethnic rebellion of blacks, Puerto Ricans, Chicanos, and recently the American Indians, has been most intense in school districts and on campuses. Women's liberation has had eager participants on the campuses. Extramarital sex by over a third of college youth replaces the small minority usually ostracized in former days. Freedom of speech and assembly since Berkeley has extended to all manner of protests and demands for redress of private grievances. Reversion to "natural" and "authentic" lifestyles extends to simple clothes, foods, houses, and recreations.

Students have engaged also in a corresponding upswing in support of activities to correct the irrationalities of traditional culture. Conclusion of the Vietnam War and revision of the draft laws were results of organized student pressure in an important degree. Concern for natural resources by the nation has been an important outgrowth of student attention to the import of biology, economics and sociology. Campus groups have voiced increasing misgivings about endowment of investments that support war production or threaten environmental pollution. Funds for research that might support defense, foster damage to ecology, or unleash genetic monsters, have come under stormy protest on many occasions.

Having confronted student protests in nearly

---

[8]_Detroit Free Press_, July 8, 1977.

every one of these categories, I have had to concede, even admire sometimes, despite the nuisance of dealing with obstructionists to the point of illegality, their noble aims at new values. Students will have some values looked out for. Such efforts to attain rights for others have actually had a significant moral vitality in the history of American democracy, as Boorstin has pointed out. Half a million mostly white soldiers died to free the slaves, and the civil rights of Negroes have been financed by Jews, Catholics and Protestants of all races. The constitutional right of women to vote was enacted by men.[9] John Dewey's dream of "education for social change" has been coming true in some important respects. The remaining questions of the cause and validity of these changes in value press for answers.

Professors have, to be sure, been involved in these value changes in one way or another. Some were among the most articulate in the crusade to make politics "moral" toward the end of the '60s. So vigorously did they concern themselves with political action that many critics have pointed to "the scandal of politicizing the university" in that period. Tolerance of differences in political values did diminish as concern for a single right answer mounted. "Affirmative action" and reform of campaign practices have emerged with specific and identifiable professorial supporters.

With the renewed willingness of students to "get involved"[10] in many other enterprises beside athletics and fraternities, the participation of professors in a wide range of value discussions must be recognized. Students do not "reform" an academic community by imposing their early values on it when they enroll.

---

[9] Daniel Boorstin, op. cit., p. 59.

[10] Cf. Robert M. Rosenzweig, "Faculty Standards of Ethical Conduct." In Sidney Hook and Miro Todorovich (Eds.), The Ethics of Teaching and Research, op. cit., pp. 73-79.

They develop them most notably within that community. Student generations come and go and their value preferences ebb and flow. The continuity element in the academic community is obviously the faculty. Its professors have the means of articulating values with students, and some interface of values must certainly be taking place.

Unfortunately this function remains spotty in its exercise, often ignored by "objective" scholarship, and uneven in its effectiveness, depending upon the interests and training of the professor. How professors can be helped to reliable, scholarly, and "objective" value cultivation constitutes the most crucial task before academe in this generation.

III

Attention to the importance and urgency for the professor's qualification to deal with value faces a down-drag from several quarters. First, opportunities for direct informal influence on students' values are not likely to increase. The structure and financing of higher education point in fact toward coming diminution of such privileges. Small colleges said to make such occasions more frequent and effective are obviously having grave financial problems, and these are not giving much promise of decline. More of such institutions may be forced to close. The prospect of benefactors creating any notable number of new colleges is almost negligible in the presence of mounting costs and declining enrollments.

Instruction of students in large numbers at sizable institutions will continue, and probably increase despite projections of zero population growth. Increasing reliance on technological aids helps to save personnel costs and "improves" instruction of large groups somewhat. But it facilitates conveyance of information largely. Exposure to values held by various people and expressed by various institutions, to be sure, can be vividly accomplished by many of these devices. But education on any sensible definition is "inconceivable unless it provides for and promotes the interaction of minds," in debate as Robert Hutchins has emphatically emphasized.[11] Value formation must be made possible somehow in formal instruction and that usually means in relatively large groups. Technological devices need to be turned largely to such means of interaction, if values, the heart of education, can claim to be the business of academe. Concern with value must show in the professor's contact with students however limited that may be.

A second factor making insistent but complicated the professor's concern with values appears in the public's growing demand for actual embodiment of them by an educational institution, and its practical assistance in value attainment. There is much to support Max Lerner's thesis that "the essence of American civilization" is "access."[12] By that he means that the recent increase in demand for access to legal protection, medical service, decent housing, full employment, and certainly to education, expresses the American belief that these values were never intended to be the exclusive privilege of the wealthy or socially elite. The genius of democracy in this country has been opportunity for all of its citizens regardless of race, social class, economic level, sex, or even ability, by some recent interpretations.

[11]"Implications for Education." In Max Kaplan and Phillip Bosserman, Technology Human Values and Leisure. New York: Abingdon Press, 1971, p. 122.

[12]"The Revolutionary Frame of Our Time." In Lawrence E. Dennis and Joseph F. Kauffman. The College and the Student. Washington: American Council on Education, 1966, p. 14. Also, The Unfinished Country. New York: Simon and Schuster, 1959.

Public scrutiny of agencies affecting these values is bound to increase. "Citizens' Groups" are here to stay. The current clogging of courts and legislatures by petitions for redress indicates a lack of rational consensus about the access to values claimed as "rights." This press by our "consumer oriented" society gives every evidence of acceleration. Though nearly all professions claim that they pursue the common good, justification of that claim is the issue in a vast body of daily news reports. An open society exposes to inspection claims to legitimacy by any or all of its service agencies and that includes the work of professors.

If professors cannot provide assistance in access to the good life what good is education, the public reasons. There are right values and professors should be made to earn their salt by showing the way to them. The retreat from education reflects an obvious discontent with the success of the teaching profession in helping students to desirable values. Aside from the legitimacy of this demand, the professor must reckon with the fact that it is being made, and it will not go away.

A third impingement on the professor's work consists in the affirmation by students of what they consider right values, whether the professor helps them to such conclusions or not. The professor's only choice is to allow student values to form willy-nilly, or to see to it that they are assisted by his competence. If the academic community is to remain "the court of last resort," a status which Walter Lippmann asserted it had traditionally maintained,[13] the professor cannot exclude from his work what students prize the most. Success, institutional authority,

---

[13]"The University and the Human Condition." In Charles G. Dobbins and Calvin B. T. Lee (Eds.), Whose Goals for American Education? Washington: American Council on Education, 1968, p. 235.

family life, recreation, art, moral virtue cannot be dismissed as the mere domain of student mores, or the private world of individual opinion.

Absence of any all-inclusive instructional and hence valuational authority has often been extolled as a paramount virtue of "the American System." With no all-embracing church, clearly defined system of social classes, fixed order of industrial production, or fully coordinated educational structure, no comprehensive system of values is affirmed by the nation as the right one. Yet every student bears with him some convictions about the right one. For a professor to write off the hodgepodge of "systems" held by students as none of his business would be intolerable.

Values form, it goes without saying, as a consequence of interaction by individuals with a wide variety of environmental stimuli. The "close" environment, the family, school, neighborhood, peer groups, ethnic associations and public media, has the most influence. Those professionally trained, and hence most capable potentially to guide value formation, should be found in the schools, and ultimately in the college and university classrooms.

This division of labor, judged at least by the time and money assigned to higher education, assumes that some essentials of the good life are attainable in the schools, despite all the variables of cultural experience, family associations, health, geography and age, the students represent. Revulsion against dictated values or required uniformity in them is bred into American democracy. It is not help in decision about what value conclusions to accept, but aid in the tools of valuation, critical judgment about the attainment and preservation of the good life, for which the public senses the professor should be held accountable.

A successful senior professor in a well-known university recently commented to me that he was increasingly doubtful whether students can manage a successful trip to a degree without the help of a psychiatrist. Instruction does have value outcomes. Are the value influences of professors that unreliable and contradictory?

There are some features of the professor's role in value formation that are reasonably obvious and commonly accepted. His credibility may certainly be judged at least by reference to his success in performing these functions, no matter what others may count.

First, the professor serves to expose students to values, hopefully as many new and varied ones as possible, without control of the result. Aside from the limits to this function set forth in Chapter Two, exposure to value remains an inevitable service up to a point. Teachers in any field have the privilege and obligation of showing the range of human experience the subjects in their discipline illuminate. They "uncover" the field more than "cover" it. Lionel Trilling found in teaching modern literature that the value interests of students was so strong as to make the creative work of writers a substitute for religion. The judgment of what is really good or evil in culture would then be conditioned by the range of data on which this judgment could rest.[14] Students are looking for the values a professor can expose.

Academic institutions commonly seek to "expose students to the first rate" by their occupational expectations of professors and the plans of study they offer. Curriculum committees and faculty meetings provide ample and notorious sport for contestants as to

---

[14] *Beyond Culture*. New York: The Viking Press, 1965, pp. 219-220.

which values should be featured. The "I have a dream" of Martin Luther King has many versions! Distinguished visitors, off-campus programs, public performances and exhibits of the arts, and even campus architecture are all intended to expose students to what matters. No one doubts this purpose of teaching, though special interests of professors often limit it.

A second characteristic of the professor's role in value detection rests in his personification of the values he prizes. Inclination toward model-formation is native the psychologists point out, as shown in children's imitation of parents, older siblings, or "best friends."[15] Students identify with leaders they approve, and hence the institution may well be concerned that what its professors stand for expresses value import worthy of student acceptance. President Eliot worried about the number of students who studied with George Santayana's naturalistic skepticism, the belief that values were ultimately identified by mere "animal faith." The number of naturalists Harvard could afford to turn out was a concern to him.

Some strong influences in the campus climate tend to minimize the admiration of "Mr. Chips," and hence to reduce the tendency of students to identify with professors. The anti-hero mode of much contemporary literature, the prominence of egocentric psychology fostered by a Freudian concern to eliminate inhibitions, depletes the effective attachments of students and their willingness to admire any other person, say nothing of professors. The sensation-battering of television and rock music, and the artificial stimulation of "high" moments by drugs sometimes dim or obscure for students the appeal of a professor's personification

---

[15] Joseph Adelson, "The Teacher as Model." In Nevitt Sanford (Ed.), The American College. New York: John Wiley & Sons, 1962, pp. 396-417.

of values. Antiseptic objectivity in scholarship, aided by the current vogue for "linguistic analysis," tends also to dissolve direct access to values person-to-person communication normally allows.

Personal conveyance of value embraced by the professor remains, nonetheless, a basic ingredient of his credibility. Symphonies without Beethoven, relativity without Einstein, civil rights without Martin Luther King, would remain uncompelling vague concepts. A professor "knows his stuff" by coming across to students as master of the import in what he says. The undoubted power of personal example in formation of moral values is a clue to the importance of the personal medium in assisting all values to come alive. One cannot imagine a student learning much about art from a professor ignorant of its essentials and disdainful of its import, as shown in the Rembrandts, Renoirs and Picassos. Such a function as value-bearer is expected of professors.

Another stage in value formation where a credible professor normally figures consists in "confrontation," or "encounter" with values involving serious choice. The chief merit in much contemporary literature lies in its stark portrayal of value systems that force the reader into a judgment about their legitimacy or merit for replication. Alex Haley's Roots demands unavoidably a reaction to the life history of his black family. Hemingway's The Old Man and the Sea calls for an appraisal of persistent struggle in the human journey. How well I remember that economics provided me with a direct encounter with value. It came with my first "A" in college when I discovered that it dealt with a "margin of utility," among other problems, in the work I was doing to earn my way through school.

Two problems complicate the confrontation with value that most people expect the professor to accomplish. First, the immediate reference to the student's lot is difficult to show in some subjects. Atomic theory is part of the architecture of science which is obviously essential in the large, but its minute refinements may seem remote. Grammar in a foreign language often seems remote to a good life. Professors working in such fields simply have a larger occupational load to carry for their success. It is just the unwillingness or ineptitude of so many professors to make encounter with values possible in their subject that leaves values such phantoms as they often are.

A second, and perhaps more serious, difficulty in bringing about meaningful encounter with values arises from the fragmented and artificial character of much student experience. When America was still largely a rural country work, play, learning, loving, worship, artistic creation, exposure to nature were all-of-a-piece. They were directly appropriated in the experience of most students. Present day students with urban heritages have only indirect knowledge of how most plants and animals grow, the way man struggles and cooperates with nature, or assists with birth of living things. Specialized studies in academic life segment even more the fragments in perceptions of "how things are." Nitrate of potassium, for example, can have a limited value for a student of chemistry in a laboratory, but reveal quite unsuspected values where observed on a farm in use as a fertilizer, or detected as a cause of pollution in drinking water along a stream.

A credible professor is the continuity piece in learning. He is a bearer of values in man's history, and manager of relations among values his students miss when left to their own pursuits. Classic illustrations of the professor at work in these services may be seen in Jacob Bronowski's The Ascent of Man,[16] or in Lewis Thomas's Lives of a Cell.[17] The first portrays with rich illus-

---

[16] Boston: Little, Brown & Company, 1973.
[17] New York: Bantam Books, Inc., 1974.

trations the development of civilization in
relation to nature, and the latter sets forth
the intricate web of relations which organisms
possess within nature. Men share, says Thomas,
with gorillas, turtles, whales, thrushes, bats
and crickets the ability to make sounds, usually with some syntax and harmonic structure,
reflecting perhaps "the ceaseless clustering
of bonded atoms into molecules of higher and
higher complexity, and the emergence of cycles
for storage and release of energy." This
process may be part of the inexhaustible flow
of energy from the sun into unfillable outer
space, but also through the earth into an increasingly ordered state of matter.[18] Such
themes of continuity tie together many valuable perspectives.

Not every course lends itself fully to
such comprehensive treatment, to be sure.
But confrontation with identifiable values
and their context is essential to vital
learning in any subject. The professor
is not only permitted to treat values in
this way, he may be expected to. In his
annual report for 1975-76 Dean Rosovsky of
Harvard College expressed the conviction
that "an educated person" is expected to
have some understanding of and experience
in thinking about moral problems, for "informed judgment" about them "may well be. . .
the most significant quality" in learning.[19]
It remains only to point out that what one
does with any value is the crux of learning.
Moral decisions cannot be made in abstraction from the whole family of values. The
professor presents the opportunity for values
to make their appeal in as comprehensible a
context as he can muster.

It is the fourth stage in value development which is the most crucial, and the most
disputed, in the professor's relation to

---

[18]Ibid., p. 27.

[19]Henry Rosovsky, "What Makes the Best College
Education?" Harvard Today, n. d., p. 8.

values, namely their "soundness" or validity.
Values are held and defended ultimately because their possessor considers them "right"
or justifiable. How far may a credible professor go in espousing "right values"? Such
values have been internalized by their holder,
i.e., they are considered defensible in the
presence of competing claims of others, and
able to bear critical scrutiny by linguistic,
cultural and logical norms. They are meaningfully related to other values and assist
comprehension of man's relation to his world.
Should the professor be required to balk when
he comes to values asserted by such standards
of valuation?

V

On the seal of nearly every institution
of higher learning there is some equivalent
of "veritas," the symbol of Harvard University. But when truth is truth, or how one
"valuable truth" relates to another, remain
standing points of issue on every campus,
when does the professor reach the true values,
answers to the sixty-four dollar questions?

For fifty years the American Association
of University Professors has fought the notion that "right values" are the possession
of any single individual, interest group, or
class of supporters sponsoring higher education. Academic freedom has become so pre-
cious because the professor's search for
truth is essentially an affirmation of right
value together with all the factors considered pertinent in support of it. The
public has a stake in the freedom to search
for and defend insights by professors which
may affect its own welfare directly, and
certainly indirectly. Professors rightly
defend from all external forces their right
to inquire after true values.

Yet, so cautious and "objective" have
some professors become in their efforts to
guard against prejudice, cultural provincial-

76

ism, cloudy logic, and wish-fulfillment, that the impression is often left either that there are no right values, or that they are matters of individual opinion. But such impressions certainly cannot follow truly from a clear conception and persistent exercise of the professor's real function. Presumably he teaches because some insights are more justifiable and hence more valuable than others. He bears the commission to espouse the sounder ones. Woodrow Wilson liked to quote Edmund Burke's declaration that "public duty demands. . .that what is right should not only be made known but made prevalent." The credible professor is a public servant in any kind of educational institution and thus he exercises both these functions.

Unless teaching is to become bankrupt of purpose, the professor's work involves him inevitably in the fate of values, and thus in the validity of qualitative judgments. The institution's obligation embraces the duty to insure that its policies are not dated, that is, hitched to one set of values popular at a given time. The crux of the issue about values in learning becomes the criteria by which staff members are chosen, supported and promoted and the means offered to assist them in performing their value function most reliably.

Paul Weiss's recommendation that learning should always be "intransitive" or committed to no single value proposition,[20] warns against narrowness of purpose and restriction in perspectives on truth. However, truth is always known as a qualitative affirmation about a particular set of circumstances. "A truly democratic president. . ." would be a meaningless proposition apart from its reference to a Jimmy Carter or a Franklin

---

[20]_Knowledge in Search of Understanding_. Mount Kisco, N. Y.: Futura Publishing Company, Inc., 1976, p. 212.

Roosevelt. There is a standing danger that valuations will be too specific, and lack the very generalization that learning ultimately needs most. "Radicals," condemned for disregard of specific values on the campus, have often become freely acceptable at later times. Angela Davis was dismissed as a communist in the '60s from UCLA, but in the spring of 1976 lectured to over a thousand at Stanford University on "The Female Condition."

But if learning is forever intransitive its origin and reliability would both be in jeopardy. Learning is about something in particular, however far its significance may range. A credible professor equips his students to apprehend values that are both timeless and timely, specific in their influence, but members also in a larger family of concepts that have import beyond the immediate present.

Respect for the integrity of individual student minds will prevent his insistence that they adopt his political, religious, aesthetic, moral, or intellectual conclusions. But he may, indeed must, insist that they perfect the techniques of establishing the reliability of values in their study of his and related fields. He does this by the way he treats and directs student handling of materials to be studied. They are the "right" ones for the purposes of the course.

Articulation and judgment of values proceeds in the weighting of alternatives and their consequences when thinking of solutions to problems. If, for example, a professor of literature treats D. H. Lawrence's Lady Chatterley's Lover as important for its authentic and sincere treatment of sex, the implications of such an interpretation need to be made explicit. The professor may be called upon legitimately to indicate the standing of sex in relation to the rest of experience, the import of Freudian assumptions about the dan-

78

gers of inhibitions, and the cultural significance of bringing language about genitals to a level of subjects not traditionally concerned with private functions. How, a credible professor would ask, is this view "better" than the alternate and traditional way of ignoring Lady Chatterley as deviant, obscene and inappropriate?

Alternative "good" answers to problems are determined by the range of generalizations, and the results which they allow, both with respect to the recurrence of similar experiences, and with regard to future time. Students need to know whether the gun is loaded which each professor invites them to handle. It is the transcendence of attention above minute particulars in experience fostered by the "explosion" of knowledge, and transcendence of the inclination of scholars to analyze problems to either-or polar conceptions, that the academic community so often lacks.

An institution has the duty to urge, even require, its professors to recognize the demands of "cloture," as the psychologists call it. Walking requires one foot to fall as the other rises, so knowledge calls for what follows from one conception to another. If euthanasia rids us of the suffering, cost and unaesthetic features of death, what does it allow with regard to the motives of heirs who might profit from it? If food and drugs are to be regulated, are the problems of regulating liquor consumption in the Volstead act to be avoided?

A professor is sometimes called "a fiduciary for the future." Learning assumes sufficiently similar circumstances tomorrow to make worthwhile study of health, vocational enterprises, extension of personal relations, clarification of political issues, and increase and guidance of sensitivity through art, and so on. The credible professor expects favorable valuation and "acceptance" of these circumstances. His excellence consists in the extent to which he enables students to claim more values, i.e., to enlarge their own being, in the up-coming future. It is this forward reference in time that learning involves, which makes cloning, invention of bombs, dissolution of marriage, or the formulation of a new utopia so crucial. Learning is an assertion of what it will be good to know tomorrow.

Far from restraining its professors from concern with right value, the house of intellect should be one in which professors are encouraged to foster true values. The contagiousness, or "fecundity" of values is a prime feature of them. Bentham's "hedonistic calculus" included emphasis not only on the intensity, duration and certainty of pleasure, but also its capacity to enrich other pleasures. Is this not an essential feature of all values? Truth when found arouses curiosity about its ramifications. The right values ramify in intelligible and defensible ways. Thomas Wolfe remembered most those professors at Harvard who invited him to the pleasures of the intellect, "the inspiration of a quickening intelligence," which he found to be the key to so many other values.[21]

Moral goodness in the non-violence of a Gandhi has inspired imitation and invention by American civil rights workers. When Isaac Stern plays a violin concert applause for an encore says in effect not only "Do it again," but also "I wish I could do that." Many an aspiring musician goes home to practice harder, and most others look further in different moments for aesthetic values Stern has suggested. John Wesley's heart was "strangely warmed" at Aldersgate, with the result that millions were influenced through his proclamation of it to worship the source of that religious value.

---

[21] You Can't Go Home Again. New York: Grosset & Dunlap, 1940, p. 710.

It is just the tenacious adherence to one
or a few values, and refusal to follow their
implications for other values, that has wrought
such havoc in our history. Economic values
made supreme as by Marxians ignores the moral,
religious, aesthetic and wide ranging other
values that root deeply in human life and also
affect its destiny. Hawthorne's story made
vivid the devastating stigma in Hester's life
when Puritan chastity was separated from values
in Christian charity. And who can forget the
brazen pursuit of "truth" about disease by Nazi
doctors while ignoring the pain and degradation inflicted on their experimental victims?

What is implied here is that the institution of learning which asserts its mission as
the exposition of "truth" rests on an inte-
grable scheme of values that professors are
expected to explore and to which their work
continuously relates. Their will-to-meaning,
essential to credibility, must assume a meaningful whole of truth if rationality has any
value or import. Claims by "structuralists"
are doubtless too rigid, that the syntactic
use of a given language within the idiom of
its culture employs "innate" or "archetypal"
patterns of reference to true reality.[22]
Variations in value import of terms, the
source of so much dispute among scholars,
remains too painfully obvious. At the same
time, intelligent discourse requires some
meaningful whole to which terms refer and
thus valuations attach, however their for-
mulations may differ.

The same cannot be said for irrationality,
or supposedly meaningless being. An irrational,
hating Joseph McCarthy brought the roof of
sanity down on his head in his senate "investi-
gations" of alleged communists. Smokers invite
lung cancer. Contradictions, frustrations of

---

[22]Cf. Daniel Patte, Structuralism, an Interdisciplinary Study. Pittsburgh: The Pickwick
Press, 1975, p. 82.

value, vague illusions have to stand in some
larger context of meaning to be understood or
even to be accurately identified. The greatest
proof of the ultimate reality of good, the
stability of value, is the instability and
partiality of evil, as Whitehead liked to
point out.

The see-saw of argument in the academic
community about true values rests on the assumption that "rational inquiry is self-cor-
rective," in Sidney Hook's terms.[23] This
self-correction can proceed however only if
professors consider that they work in the same
house of intellect or whole of truth, and do
not give equal footing to those ideas which
make intelligible discourse itself impossible.
The institution needs continuously to reempha-
size this conception of singleness and totality
in its scheme of values for its professors to
gain and retain credibility.

Efforts to gain more cohesion in learning
have been made through "interdisciplinary"
studies that have recently become popular.
Many of these efforts have been fruitless
and superficial, or even more confusing because of the multiplicity of subjects treated.
The root problem in most cases lies in lack of
preparation by participating faculty members
to think in terms of each other's values. My
role at the National Endowment for the Humanities, intimately associated with aid to some
of these programs, leads me to mention some.

At the University of Illinois, for example, an effort has been made to develop
the value implications of major subjects. A
trial run was made by a seminar on "Problems
of the Economic-military Complex." Professors
from the economics, political science, philosophy and engineering departments were participants. They considered it a failure in in-

---

[23]Sidney Hook and Miro Todorovich, <u>The Ethics
of Teaching and Research</u>. <u>Op</u>. <u>cit</u>., p. 120.

tercommunication and confusing to students. An
observer would have to conclude that too little
time was spent in preparation by the professors
for the interrelation of concepts, the inter-
weaving of values. The magnitude of the problems in developing a common universe of discourse, the focus of value in the whole of truth,
is illustrated here. Unless the institution believes such efforts important enough to spend
time and money on them, they are bound to slip
back into the atomism characteristic of most
curricula.

A successful illustration of such efforts
at coherence in learning has been provided by
Albion College. Ten established professors
representing the departments of English, speech,
biology, mathematics, philosophy, religion,
psychology and economics were excused from
teaching one three hour class each for two
semesters in order to take part in a seminar
of their own. Their commission was to search
for any concepts, values, or themes, which
interpenetrate the learning community. They
found the common coin of thinking in such a
setting to consist of those ideal values, or
"basic ideas" which are essential for inquiry
and discourse concerning man's understanding
of himself, his society, his relation to
nature, and his formulation of values. Each
professor thereafter for two years taught one
section of students in the experimental group,
studying each of these four realms of "basic
ideas."

Elaborate tests by off-campus authorities revealed that students in this program
"matured" about a year earlier than those
not so enrolled. Their capacity to analyze
problems, deal with prejudice, identify
values, and initiate their own studies was
markedly higher. But the effect on the participating faculty was even more significant.
One professor, previously accustomed to extensive publication of studies in psychology
dealing with miniscule factors in learning,

declared it "the most important educational experience of my life." No professor was less competent in his specialty thereafter, but more competent in grasp of its context. The program has become a permanent part of the curriculum.

At Hastings-on-Hudson the Institute of Society, Ethics and Life Sciences has been working diligently on problems of value in education, chiefly at graduate and professional levels. Instigated by leaders in medical ethics, the Center has invited contributions to ethics in teaching by professors from all over the country. Progress is being made in devising courses in ethics, though the broader problem of how all professors affect the value life of students does not appear yet to be addressed.[24]

Beneath the expectation by an academic institution that it will qualify students for success in a special profession, turn out "good citizens," release new levels of genius, contribute to the advance of culture, must lie qualification in use of tools for valuation. Learning will continue to generate divisiveness, narrowness of purpose, myopia of aim, declining interest in intellectual things, unless the institution insists that its professors find some cohesive belief system within which their several endeavors retain some kinship. "Right values" do not drop into a professor's or a student's mind from heaven. They may be held legitimately only after rigorous pursuit which is subject to informed criticism of colleagues.

VI

Will the academic community learn to qualify students to draw the pucker string of values in their education? Or will this be left to the haphazard pulling and hauling of politicians, advertisers, evangelists, gurus, or demagogues?

---

[24]Address by Director of the Center, Daniel Callahan, "Ethics and Value Education." Association of American Colleges, Washington, D. C., Feb. 8, 1978.

It is a sober prospect for democracy to con-
template the continuing neglect of values in
learning by higher education. They attach to
learning inevitably, but their bearing on the
outlook of students by a course of inquiry, the
cohesion among them, and their articulation by
scholars in the total realm of intelligible discourse, remains so far a massive hodge-podge.

For institutions of learning, the supposed
centers of leadership in American society, to
tolerate such heterogeneity only augments the
confusions of democracy. If academe remains a
cross-section of society rather than providing
a model for society, it only continues to be
an accessory to the fact of "the downfall of
the west." American life is already dazzled
by the ideals of freedom in speech and action,
and the right of privacy in pursuit of happiness. The "little catechism of natural rights"
has been allowed to obscure the common stake in
loyalties and values self-government makes
necessary.[25]   Unless the academic community
provides a counteracting agency to these centrifugal forces, the disintegration of "the open
society" is a sure promise. The house of intellect dare no longer remain divided against
itself.

Some value-oriented institutions that have
had powerful effects on history remind us of
the role articulated values can have, whatever
one thinks of the schemes they expressed.

Scholasticism rested on orthodox, tightly
knit ideological systems provided by theology,
the queen of the sciences, until nearly the
middle of the twentieth century. Now we know,
of course, that scientific research, progress
of civil rights, and the multiplication of knowledge and education have undermined these monolithic systems. Today Catholics are becoming
less and less distinguishable from Protestant

----

[25]Harold Brody, The Politics of South Africa. New
York: Oxford University Press, 1977. Closing
paragraphs of the last chapter.

and even secular thinkers. Whatever the gains through growth in individual authority for modern thinkers, the fact remains that the scholastic rule of belief and practice saved western civilization from the devastating barbarians.

Today Russian totalitarianism retains control at least officially of the educational and cultural aspirations of its people. The Pasternaks, Solzhenitsyns and Mnyukhs shout to the rest of the world that communist goals of social morality and justice, as well as national growth and security, smother the individuality and creativity of Russian people. It remains a matter of record, however, that illiteracy has been reduced from 50 to 5% in the last 30 years, and the number of doctors increased from 20,000 to 300,000. The productivity and military might of the country have grown to such mighty proportions as to affect the foreign policy of nearly every other nation, and the internal policy of many.

It may be anathema to suggest that such totalitarian and all-inclusive value systems can be instructive to our country, with its laissez-faire system of allowing values to flower where they will. But can the devastating divisiveness of urban life be continued? Can the sectional and special interests of lobbies that dominate Congress equip American democracy to endure in the presence of developing nations with world-wide influence? Can the lawlessness that mounts go on? Can the ineffectiveness of much education augur well for tomorrow?

Insistence by an educational institution that search for and articulation of values be its basic purpose need not result in a monolithic cultural structure. Belief that there are "true values" and assistance in articulation of them without dictation of conclusions about them, will remain an operation that is free-wheeling enough! Thinking itself generates looseness among values for intellectual activity is not imitation of someone else's perspective. A value is the grasp by a person of the import in a separate perspective that is personally claimed. To think a conclusion "true," or an action "good," is to affirm a direction of thought by a separate individual. The cohesion of these separate perspectives remains the assumption of the "truth" claimed by any one of them. It will speak for itself if invited.

Political democracy allows independent thought but it cannot go on doing so without insisting that its participants seek some coordination and cohesion in values which make trustworthy their individual decisions. Protection and cultivation of a community of ideas and values is essential to a stable and civilized society. If it does not exercise this function to the maximum, there will be "No Exit," for hell, as Sartre pointed out, will be "other people." American institutions will not stand the bombardment of politically organized agents indifferent to free-standing values. The agencies which assist independence of judgment will be betrayed into failure of their reason for being.

CHAPTER FOUR

ATLAS AND THE PROPHET

I

Concern by a professor with values focuses his
work on the kind of future thought desirable. Does
the teacher "affect eternity," as Henry Adams
claimed? Certainly no professor could obtain
credibility if his teaching went out of date at
sundown the day it was given. Learning is "future
scanning" for it is pursued in the expectation of
its value for ensuing circumstances. Yet, no one
knows with certainty much in detail about tomorrow's
circumstances. One of the greatest paradoxes of the
professor's work is that he must guide thought for
the future as if he knew what cannot be fully known.

Most commonplace conduct, however, is organized
around expectations that this paradox is not genuine,
for tomorrow will be like today in many respects.
One learns the table of chemical elements, or the
provisions of the constitution, for example, in
the belief that chemical analysis of nutrients
in foods will be valid, and responsibilities of
public officials binding in a foreseeable and
reliable future. The future is "prologue" to
present action, even more than "the past is prologue," for its conception provides the reason
for learning.[1]

A professor deserves credibility whose teaching promises to "do you good," succeeds in it as
the future unfolds, and presumably does the most
good in the longest future. Facility in foretelling values in thought and action for times
not yet present inheres by definition in the
teacher's function. A professor puts before
students the belief that the quality of the
future, and therefore of their own future,

---
[1]Cf. Wendell Bell, "Futuristics and Social Behavior."
In Robert Bundy (Ed.), Images of the Future. Buffalo:
Prometheus Books, 1976, p. 57.

can be shaped in at least some important ways by
their learning.

Perhaps the greatest confusion and wildest
speculation about any part of higher education
have surrounded its inevitable thrust toward the
future. Many writers have "dipt into the future,
far as human eye could see" and discerned much
more detail than Tennyson could in "Locksley
Hall." Orwell's "Big Brother" and Huxley's
"World Controller" have been conjured as emerging agencies of thought and behavior control.
Manipulation of genes to alter heredity, brain
surgery to pacify troublesome people, subhuman
sources for spare parts to repair the human
body, to say nothing of "Superman" and "The Six
Million Dollar Man," have been having varying
degrees of fascination, admiration, fear, and
credibility.

In this scientific and realistic age, we
are all sternly warned by recognized scholars
that knowledge must be "verified" to be believed.
Yet, a blunt disregard of the future, separation
of actual events from possible and probable
events, is not "scholarly" either. Judgment of
what is valuable, and thus worthy of belief,
runs ahead into future projection. "The way
it is" shades over into "the way it's going to
be" in at least some important degree. This
"day" means a time-span of light that will re-
cur tomorrow, else the term is meaningless.
I believe scholarship must include projection
of future values it serves or destroys.

Concern with future conditions is certainly
fascinating, and it is also practical as well as
a basis for obligations. The mystery yet fascination of the future lies at the heart of much
literature and art. Mystery stories clearly
enthrall their readers by the uncertain "way it
will all turn out." Much other imagination in
the arts also holds attention by its concern
with what <u>can</u> happen, or how one in future should
conceive or feel about what <u>has</u> happened.[2]   Scien-

---
[2] John C. Cawelti, <u>Adventure, Mystery, and Romance</u>.

tific research of a Pasteur, Curie or modern cancer researcher often seems driven by a deeply placed "instinct" demanding secrets of the future more than any other reward.[3]

Millions of dollars spent on "research and development" in business and government rests on the practical value of projecting future conditions. Publication of the price index, balance of trade, or unemployment figures for a given period have a direct effect on the stock market, and on some legislation, for both business and government are concerned in practice with what can and should happen in the future.

This involvement with the future has its most important feature in the obligations man accepts, for duties concern pursuit of values not possessed. If man does not consciously try for future values they will be determined for him by others, by nature, or by chance combination of these factors. Human beings become fully human by their power to imagine the future and to work for its most valuable features.[4] Response to obligation is the measure of fulfillment in this capacity.

Preoccupation with "inquiry" in the academic community often seems to make admiration of insight and "new knowledge" intrinsic values. But since the consequences of knowing involve its use or disuse, improvement or impairment of the human lot, pursuit of future knowledge impinges on the present. The responsible scholar must carry with him an "ultimate concern" for the future of humanity, for his knowledge will be a part of that future. Like food, knowledge nourishes, poisons or merely provides bulk to the digestive future of the body. To ignore

Chicago: The University of Chicago Press, 1976, pp. 42-43, 16-17.

[3]Lewis Thomas, The Lives of a Cell. New York: Bantam Books, 1974, pp. 118-119.

[4]Fred L. Polak, "Responsibility for the Future." In Robert Bundy, op. cit., pp. 13, 10.

the effects of learning on man's future is as
disastrous as to pay no attention to the effects of food on the body.

Willingness to be a parasite on concern
by others for values in the future is degenera-
tive of human qualities. Our ancestors have
made it possible for America to enjoy richer
material comforts, and cultural as well as artistic perceptions, beyond those of any past
dreams, and surpassing a large majority of
other nations. Concern for the kind of future
we leave our children is, however, rarely
thought out. John Adams rightly predicted:
"Posterity! You will never know how much it
cost the present generation to preserve your
freedom."[5] The divisions and corruption among
some political leaders, strife of labor and ethnic groups, and the dominance of corporations
driven by the appetite for present profits,
imply the belief that some future individuals
or institutions should supply these groups
with the privilege to pursue their selfish
interests. Part of a credible professor's
job is to focus his students' efforts on realization of values that will enhance their own
humanity, not sap the strength of others who
believe man's future as man is more than a
private concern.

Projections about the future have varying
success. Terms like "alienation," "disorienta-
tion," "frustration," "nihilism," so commonly
used to characterize this age, point to predictions by cultural leaders, including some
professors, that have failed. Some of Nietzsche's predictions, on the other hand, have
come to pass. His forecast in 1888 (The Will
to Power) that rational calculation as manifest in modern science would lead to Nihilism,
the collapse of cultural aspirations, seems
to describe much of the contemporary scene, in
the opinion of a sober number of observers.

---

[5]Adams Papers. Massachusetts Historical Society,
Boston, Mass.

Two trends seem to support Nietzsche's conviction. One is the decline of belief in progress,
as control seems hopeless over inflation, racial
hatred, poverty, crime and political conflict.
A second factor consists in the growing conviction
in the West that affluence, with its power to
provide better diet, miracle medicine, new technology and massive production, does not bring inevitable lasting happiness, family and social
stability, or mental health. The values of Western civilization are not so self-evident as they
seemed two generations ago now that their material
resources are proving to be limited.[6]

In the face of these faltering conceptions
of the future what should be the stance of a
credible professor? Should he think of himself,
and hence of all cultural leaders, as modern
Atlases bearing the hopes of survival with forti-
tude, while the kaleidoscope of change takes
successive turns? Heilbroner believes one can
do no better.[7]   And Michael Maccoby holds that
it would even be "immoral" to try to do more by
predicting the future, for it would reduce the
obligation of man to mature his powers of invention as new needs arise.[8]

Neither Atlas nor the parasite on predictions by others in the unfolding of history
leaves the professor a credible and necessary
function. Without a professor's help our generation can grit its teeth and wait, if Atlas
be our role; or experiment to test our powers
to improvise as we go, if "gamesmanship" is
our only resource. But a blind man tapping
with his cane inspires pity not credibility.
Yet neither of these views of the future gives
credence that is any more positive to a professor.

---

[6]Robert L. Heilbroner, The Human Prospect. New York:
W. W. Norton & Company, Inc., 1974, pp. 15, 133.

[7]Ibid., pp. 143-144.

[8]The Gamesman. New York: Simon & Schuster, 1976.

A benefactor, whom I once guided to make a
major gift to the college over which I presided,
declared that he believed his lifetime spanned
the best period in American history. Still, he
gave his estate largely to higher education,
evidently in the belief that the future could
and must be better. He unconsciously manifested
in his gifts, as he had in his business, that
the vitality of American civilization has come
from its exploring spirit, its willingness to
move into the unexplored future, in the belief
that it can be meaningful and superior to the
present. If a professor is to serve a valuable
function in this civilization, he can do no less
than provide it with rational guidance, a
thoughtful projection of values worthy of
future pursuit, and promise of actual attaina-
bility.

The credible professor is a rational prophet who leads the way in building cantilever
bridges over the chasm of an "unknown," i.e.,
not yet experienced future. He does so in the
calculated conviction that his projections will
be met by some counter projections of reality
from the other side of the present. He empha-
sizes "the existential moment," as any sane
person must. But far from staring at it
stoically, bearing glumly its burdens, leaving irresponsibly its fate to blind men tapping
their canes, he projects values worthy of pursuit tomorrow. This is the obligation and
privilege of intelligence. As one with highly
trained intelligence, the credible professor
accepts the responsibilities of his post,
knowing that without him his generation wastes
its efforts or succumbs to its fears. He knows
with Robert Frost that,

> "The woods are lovely, dark and deep,
> But I have promises to keep,
> And miles to go before I sleep.
> . . . ."

The professor keeps his promises to reliable
values, however dark and deep the present

distractions, and despite the ambiguousness of future goods and goals.

II

A credible professor's identity, his true character I suppose, emphasized in Chapter Two, must include confrontation of the future, and facility in establishing values which his discipline can help reach. Philip Werdell rightly advises that, "only those who have gained confidence in their own identity and direction can create healthy future goals for society."[9] Knowledge advances to wisdom when it is "about man as he might be."[10] Unless the professor has some clear notion of what man may become and focuses his studies on at least some means to realize that condition, why should students bother with such teaching?

As the search for a successor to Kingman Brewster as President of Yale proceeded, the uncertainty came to light of many professors about the purpose of their profession as well as their status at Yale. During the administrative change one professor was reported to say, "The Yale faculty has a sense it isn't doing something important any more. There's a lack . . .of purpose about what you're doing and its value."[11] A professor who cannot see the value of his work in realizing a meaningful future for himself and his students is certainly a liability to the society which has assigned him just that function.

While students thrash about, trying on various identities for size in hope of finding one that fits, their uncertainties need help

---

[9]"Futurism and the Reform of Higher Education." In Alvin Toffler (Ed.), Learning for Tomorrow. New York: Vintage Books, 1974, p. 286.

[10]Howard Mumford Jones, One Great Society. New York: Harcourt, Brace & Company, 1959, p. 99.

[11]The Washington Post, Oct. 25, 1977, Sec. A, p. 7.

from professors who know who they are and where
they are going. Bedeviled by the overchoice of
an affluent society, college youth fear selection of one set of values will exclude another
even more rewarding.[12] Meanwhile the constric-
tion of choice about one's future, exerted by
massive business and government, even as the
status of democracy in the world declines, con-
tributes to the fear that no one can project
successfully a role in upcoming history.[13]

Basic in academe's rationale has always
been the conviction, however, that it can help
each generation "find its own intelechy,"[14]
i.e., path into the future among its immovables
and despite its uncertainties. The credible
professor capable of reckoning with the future
performs this service by concern with values in
at least three ways.

First, he helps students identify and
articulate the values of their prevailing culture. He may have to appear as the defender
of "things as they are" to make students aware
of the values they've grown up with and have
been shaped by. A maturing adolescent needs
"something to push against" to flex and toughen
his valuational fiber, as Bettelheim points out.[15]
The student, asked to write out the Pledge of
Allegiance, who rendered the phrase "this nation
under guard," provides a pathetic glimpse of the

[12]Lionel Trilling, "The Uncertain Future of the
Humanistic Educational Ideal." The American Scholar, 44:1 (Winter, 1974-75), p. 66.

[13]Robert L. Heilbroner, The Future as History. New
York: Grove Press, Inc., 1960, p. 209.

[14]Daniel Bell, The Reform of General Education. New
York: Columbia University Press, 1966, p. 146.

[15]Bruno Bettelheim, "The Problem of Generations." In
Eric H. Erikson (Ed.), The Challenge of Youth. New
York: Anchor Books, 1965, p. 92.

inchoate condition of many of their values. Groping by students on sex, work, patriotism, art or religion reflects the indecision of many parents and teachers who don't know where they stand on these values, and have had nothing to recommend.

A second task in preparing students to search reliably for values in the future is to aid them in testing the durability of values their elders _have_ espoused. Their natural curiosity and desire for autonomy facilitate this undertaking. It usually takes little coaching to sensitize students that "something is rotten in Denmark" when economic injustice, racial disharmony, military action, or even a cold war, threaten their own plans for the future. But so much more is essential than the typical student disdain of the establishment, the corporate world, Wall Street, or Scarsdale. Failure in our time to reach stable family, religious, political, or economic values calls for decisions about legitimacy, the effects of each type of value if it were to be realized, and the condition of _all_ members of society in which given values are pursued.

Talk about the "identity crisis" and the "generation gap" must be translated into the "fidelity search" by students for "something or somebody to be true to." This groping for something to be faithful to shows in the appeal of "scientific method," "sincerity of convictions," "honesty in telling it like it is," "genuineness of human relations," "fairness" in the game, "authenticity" in art or "insight" in religion.[16] The most poignant yearning of students is for credible help in weighing such values, for they are basic to the identity students hope to carry into the future. A credible professor seeks not necessarily to close the generation gap, though that may happen in treatment of some values, but to provide guidance through it.

---

[16]Eric H. Erikson, "Youth, Fidelity and Diversity." Op. cit., pp. 24-25.

There is more division of opinion about the third task of the credible professor than perhaps any other. It consists in the need for the professor to persuade students that they can't keep their options open indefinitely. The irreversible time flow of history relentlessly makes up a student's life for him, if he lets values go by default. Marriage, work, citizenship are parts of the future whose values can be affected, or go by default according to a student's initiative.

Every student wants to "be himself," to make his own life, to build self-respect. Past disavowal of responsibility for values in learning by professors means a willingness to take at face value the student's notion of selfhood. The "fellow-feeling" emphasized in much current teaching may encourage some rapport with students. But its implied recognition of the validity in each student's choice of selfhood as his right, vacates, as we have seen, the essence of teaching as a value transaction. It is certain also that students soon lose their willingness to "collaborate" with a professor who is unable and unwilling to grapple with the status of values in the future.

Saul Bellow pointed out in his address upon receiving the Nobel prize for literature that human beings can't "bear too much unreality."[17] Effective and persistent learning by students can't bear much unreality, or "irrelevance" they call it. This "reality" in learning is the cargo of value it bears. A credible professor's "shared dream," his lodestone of values for the future, needs to come before students with a sense of urgency that their plans for the future should take cognizance of its onrush now. A professor has a stake in his students' future. He cannot discharge his duty to them if he neglects to search for defensible future values, or fails to urge their serious consideration in relation to present decisions.

---

[17]The American Scholar, 46:3 (Summer, 1977), p. 323.

This forward pitch of the credible professor's
work toward the future is easier no doubt to conceive in general, than to implement in specific
studies. But the credible professor cannot dodge
the ramifications of any subject. A professor of
chemistry, for example, must deal with principles
that promise to be valuable hypotheses for indefinite verification in the future. He must show
the import, and thus the limits as well as benefits, of using chemical frames of reference. In
dealing with such questions as pollution, involved in use of coal for energy, he shows the
relation of chemical changes to biological and
moral issues and thus to the value implications
of smoke in the atmosphere. He sets forth these
views in such form as will be intelligible to
the community affected. Such fanning out of import in chemistry strains unfortunately the usual
professor's competence.

American scholarship has reversed the outlook of the Enlightenment, whereby solution to
problems in general was believed possible to
the rational mind, without regard to specific
problems in particular. Today research is considered capable of solving almost any problem
in particular without regard to any broad problems in general.[18]   The truly basic problems
of any generation are the broad ones involving
the common welfare, or fate of values, in a
society's future.

III

When choosing professors, I have always
been concerned about their degree of modesty,
for it reveals their consciousness of what has
gone before them in the scholarly world. A
credible professor must formulate viable future
values to an important extent by reference to
history already made. To judge what values are,
which features of them deserve preservation, and

-----

[18] Gray L. Dorsey, "Rationality in the Contemporary
University." In Sidney Hook et. al. (Eds.), The
Idea of a Modern University. Buffalo: Prometheus
Books, 1974, pp. 119-120.

certainly to fashion new ones, requires knowledge
of what has been important in past events.

As citizens of the future it is sometimes
said that we are like travelers to a foreign
country needing a passport. Any person is a
complex of experiences in which the values held
have guided the configuration of past conduct.
Paul Goodman's contention that youth have been
made to "grow up absurd" by the primacy assigned to roles, prestige and profit by their
progenitors,[19] points to the importance for
professors of their value orientation in the
past. In assessing students' value orientation professors affirm their own, drawn from
their peculiar experience among those of all
other men making up past history. A professor must make sure he has not grown up absurd.

Formation of normative values by a credible
professor is complicated by the fact that "special interests" have so often colored periods
of history. The Church has often sought to
limit "dangerous values" by invoking "higher
truths." Galileo was condemned for questioning a theistic cosmology; Darwin was resisted
for espousing the evolutionary origin of man,
and Freud for asserting the prominence of sex
in human nature. Certainly political authorities
have constricted some values, from the death of
Socrates for corrupting youth, through Nazi pro-
hibition of non-Aryan physics, social science
and art, and Stalin's outlawing of theories at
variance with dialectical materialism. Contemporary counter-culture is a vocal special
group rejecting logic and empirical study in
favor of values in feeling, and the sub-rational
powers of astrology, spiritualism, exorcism and
other forms of non-science.

Selection by a professor of durable values
among these special emphases is the more crucial because a sense of history develops rela-

---

[19] Paul Goodman, Growing Up Absurd. New York:
Vintage Books, 1960, p. xiii.

tively late in life.[20]   Students haven't lived
long enough to gain a reliable perspective on
the history of the race. The "now generation"
has been accentuating this responsibility of
the professor. By denigrating the perspective
they cannot possibly possess, students leave
the professor with a task to bring to bear on
scholarship in his field a grasp of values that
only an adult can have, and without which students must muddle through each era as it comes.

Who can doubt that intelligible thought
derives much of its substance from history,
despite Henry Ford's notorious assertion that,
"History is bunk?" A professor's teaching is
drawn from his grasp of history in the very
identification of facts, events, processes, or
persons by terms that have an acceptable or un-
derstandable meaning. Words and symbols are
used because of recognized values, i.e., import, they manifest in dealing with their subjects. So "Hamlet" may be chosen for study of
"tragedy," as known to be such a losing conflict between values of loyalty to his father
and the expected fidelity of a "good" mother.
Concepts in the discussion are drawn from a
storehouse of already known references or symbols of meanings about such conflicts.

Further, selection of categories for dealing with a subject are drawn from their experienced (i.e., historical) value in explana-
tion of such problems. When civil rights are
considered, the inevitable psychological categories come up. Forms of thought come into
play stipulating whether they are inherent
"endowment by a creator," mere fiction, or
social convenience. Ethical categories involving the values of "life," "pursuit of
happiness," property, and learning are inevitable. Political categories must be used
to deal with the arrangements by a state to
care for or neglect these rights. These and

----

[20]Kenneth Eble, _Professors as Teachers_. San Francisco: Jossey-Bass, Inc., Publishers, 1972, p. 80.

other categories of thought are chosen for their values shown in past experience to be helpful in dealing with such problems.

Ultimately the ontology, the standing or reliability, of such knowledge about civil rights, comes to a showdown. Unless we are willing to throw up our hands and say, "Who knows?" the assumption that some "good" or "right" answer, at least for present circumstances in history, must be maintained. Just as Churchill's defiance of Hitler was judged by the civilized world to be "good," belief that civilization can be guided by some valid knowledge of rights comes to the fore in discussion of civil rights. A professor ventures to discuss the subject of rights because he believes man's past experience with knowledge of the subject has had some validity or value.

Though learning draws so much of its material from history, it is the fact that the wrong values in selection of facts, or deduction from those facts, so often occurs that constitutes much human bafflement, even chaos. Instruction or "lessons" from history about the course of human action are extremely difficult to discern.[21] Viewed in the large, history is a congeries of events, some chaotic and some in configuration, some predictable and others forming complete surprises. The Romans of the first century could certainly not have predicted the Catholic church, nor Marx in the nineteenth century modern totalitarian and industrialized Russia. Deduction from Dewey's philosophy that learning is best done by doing has contributed to much fuzziness and consequent dissatisfaction with public education that he never foresaw.

Yet, a major test of the right to teach consists of facility in judgment of those factors in history which comprise reliable guides

---

[21] Will and Ariel Durant, The Lessons of History. New York: Simon and Schuster, 1968, pp. 97, 13.

for future values. Some exponents of "the new history," like Carl Becker, conclude: "Every man his own historian," since what has happened, and what to make of it is so often obscure. But such personal reactions to history are often as superficial and simplistic as taking the story of the cherry tree to be a reliable index to George Washington's character. Relativism in assigning private values to history results in the collapse of reliable scholarship on any subject, as well as about history.[22]

Any teacher makes value assumptions about the relation of his discipline and its materials to past history. One cannot avoid the question of whether history repeats itself or progresses. Do the forces of nature hinder, help, or ignore the status of the human species? Is there "a divinity that shapes our ends, rough-hew them how we will," in Arnold's phrase? None of these questions is capable of exact answers, but each shapes, or at least influences, the direction of a teacher's work. A Marxian professor, for example, believing in the ultimate fashioning of human motives by economic forces, provides a much different idea of professional success than a Christian who affirms the ability of persons to respond to other motives, such as devotion to the welfare of depressed people.

Inexact answers to these large questions have fully as much, and often in important degrees more, influence on the direction of civilization as exacter answers to little questions of much "research." Some supposedly exact and "scientific" answers to little questions, for example, the penetrability of the atom before Planck and Bohr, have been false too, for that matter. And if it be objected that there are no "little questions," it is the more clear that the scheme of values guiding the scholar

---

[22]Gertrude Himmelfarb, "Observations on Humanism and History." In Sidney Hook, et. al. (Eds.), The Philosophy of the Curriculum. Buffalo: Prometheus Books, 1975, pp. 81-87.

in his use of history needs inspection. Credibility even about answers to little questions cannot rest on small dimensions, for every event has a context bearing on its meaning.

The rootage of scholarship in past experience and the selection of values it involves while future values are determined, does not invite the "historicism" Robert Nisbet fears. The academic community does not thereby become a mere "developing entity."[23] Some "development" is indeed integral to academia as new persons find new truth and new conditions raise fresh questions. But the integrity of that community, the credibility of its professors, does not dissolve with differing perspectives. "Truth" has survived many diverse "casts at eternity," as Loren Eiseley called the work of scholars, for all the centuries of recorded history. Otherwise man's transcendence of animal existence would be inexplicable.

A credible professor, knowing that he cannot avoid the historical origins of his own values and those of his discipline, strives for as articulate, orderly, and justifiable or defensible ones as his powers permit.

IV

Faculty meetings manifest their widely known volatility mainly because of the clash of nostrums about the future of students (when parking problems, pensions and academic freedom have had their inning). Such diversity about the goals of learning and their qualification for the future is a major occupational hazard for the professor.

Tools for dealing reliably with values held in the past, and deserving to be preserved, have been more fully developed, and hence are more reliable, than those dealing with the future. A credible professor is more likely to be able to deal with past his-

---

[23] _The Degradation of the Academic Dogma._ New York: Basic Books, Inc., 1971, p. 212.

tory than with the history still to be made. "Futurology" today is much more of a no-man's land than historiography.

A dramatic proliferation of "future oriented" courses reflecting efforts at a new "scientism," has stirred the imagination of many academic communities in recent years. They have also in many cases generated irresponsible fear of "future shock," the anxiety about surprise disasters. Alvin Toffler's breathless portrayal of the need of "adhocacy," a readiness for all contingencies in the post-industrial age, if education is to escape being "anti-adaptive,"[24] is an illustration.

Though the play element in the mind, represented by simulation games, brainstorming, science fiction and utopias, deserves exercise, it is important for the professor, who remains credible, not to panic. He distinguishes, first of all, possibilities from predictions. The book of Revelation, 1984, or Brave New World create havoc when taken as prediction of fact. Second, the reliable professor fulfills the most pressing need who helps find qualitative improvement for man and not mere quantitative change. To prescribe more people, more production, more government for the future only compounds problems already overwhelming.

Above all, the credible professor will face the future armed with the principle that whatever changes are to emerge, they will be possible only because of the permanent and persisting factors to which they relate. Change would be unintelligible in history as it would in a physical substance if nothing persisted.[25] The hydrogen and oxygen in water as a liquid do not vanish when frozen into a solid or evaporated into a gaseous state. Forecasts of values available in the future, or worthy of pursuit, must be made within

---

[24]Future Shock. New York: Random House, Inc. (Bantam Books), 1970; Learning for Tomorrow. New York: Vintage Books, 1974. Chapter I.

[25]Herbert J. Muller, "Education for the Future." The American Scholar, 41:3 (Summer, 1972), p. 353.

the framework of some persisting factors which
lead to them.

Among these permanent elements, perhaps
the most obvious is a physical environment per-
vaded by a finely tuned ecosystem on which organic, including human, life depends. Values
in access to fresh air, sunshine, pure water,
open space, fertile soil, growing plants, and
moderate sound levels, not to say periodic
silence, are prerequisites to health. Happily
this generation has awakened to the hazards of
tampering with such given conditions. A "silent
spring," empty oil wells, stinking ghettoes,
and starving third world hordes are specters
that signify a disregard of physical nature
that can be threats to survival. Not whether
nature will exist, but how men will respond
to its demands and conserve its powers is the
question for a credible professor to help
answer.

Within these demands the probability is
strong that the size, strength, sensitivity
and health needs of the human body will per-
sist in essentially the same form for thousands
of years. Alterations in these bodily factors
now possible, or soon to be achieved through
cloning, create so far counterbalancing or even
insuperable problems.[26] Climates with their
varying powers to support life, change only im-
perceptibly. Another ice age, if it ever
comes, would be aeons away. Communications
with, and even transportation to, other planets
may occur, but such developments can have only
minor effect on the course of earthly history,
if moon exploration is a reliable sample.

Second, the irremovable necessity of social and political institutions with authority
transcending private purposes will continue as
a sine qua non of civilized history. Rousseau's
"general will" is a fiction apart from social
agents to express and enforce it. A "withering

---

[26]Cf. the digest of Vance Packard's The People Shap-
ers, (published by Little, Brown and Company) in The
Saturday Review, June 20, 1977, pp. 35-48.

away of the state" predicted by Marx could, even if possible, only result in a human traffic jam transcending the wildest dreams of anarchy. Individuality essential to civilization will go on requiring efficacious social mechanisms to protect its safety, preserve its property, secure the justice and measure of equity each man seeks and believes his due. Cohesion beyond the centrifugal force of "the new ethnicity remains also an inextinguishable need.[27] Unloving critics and uncritical lovers of these social structures remain threats to their viability. But they cannot consign them to the ash can.

Another feature of the persisting framework of history is its unavoidable system of interdependent production and distribution of goods. Such a scheme is essential to attainment of more and more uniquely human properties. Though the minimum needs for nutrition, health, literacy, and culture are moving targets in different parts of the world, they provide rallying points in every society. Use of technological aides to reach "more equality" between the overprivileged and the dispossessed will remain inevitably a major enterprise by both groups for the indefinite future. Primitive societies, futilely imitated by recent communes, are gone forever. Their simple organization with lowered psychological pressures stemming from reliance on tradition and the wisdom of elders, do not fit this fast moving age of world interdependence, nor will they in any age to come.

A less tangible, but no less real, feature of continuing history will be the arrangements for a skylight of human experience to receive man's "inaudible instruction." The propensity to create literature and art, to play, hope, recoil from evil, sense the comic, admire greatness, and to feel dependent on destiny,

---

[27]Cf. Howard F. Stein and Robert F. Hill, "The Limits of Ethnicity." The American Scholar, 46:2 (Spring, 1977), p. 188.

or some plan of "transcendent good," is universal and irrepressible. The hitherto inde-
structibility of the Jewish faith, and the
historic rebellions against autocracy serve
as paradigms for the spiritual aspirations
of all people. These feelings rise and fall,
reappear and flower in many ages, whether the
course of culture in German or Russian totalitarianism, or the mysticism of American Indians, be considered.

Can anyone seriously deny the inevitability
of such furniture for the future? Premillenial-
ists try to, but even they are usually thrifty
and unwilling "to take no thought for tomorrow."
The fear of "the end of the world" lurks in the
background of frequent conversations, but who
really believes it to be more than a figure of
speech? Nuclear explosions could wipe out large
sections of the civilized world. But the total
extinction of all human life is inconceivable.
In any case, limitation on nuclear testing currently discussed gives some promise of adoption
for the sheer survival of man, let alone preservation of political superpowers.

Prospect for change more dramatic, and
unrelated to persisting values, than those in
the past century should strike the knowledgeable professor as extremely unlikely. While
I grant that we all instinctively fear radical
change, and whistle while hoping the future
will not get out of hand, I see little prospect of that happening. Rene Dubos points out
that the drama of some past events has been as
great as any conceivable future ones. In the
period of twenty-five years between the fall of
the Bastille and Waterloo political changes
shook the world. From 1850 to 1890 the development of railroads, steamships, electricity,
telephones, radios, antiseptics and surgery
was as spectacular for the period as anything
likely to come. World communication, space
exploration and the revolutions in Russia and
China provide changes unlikely to be surpassed

in radical dimensions,[28] at least within the future where present plans can have an effect.

A credible professor cannot predict many future events in detail, but he can assume some such persisting conditions within which he can foresee those values likely to be attainable, and hence those worthy of pursuit. His paramount responsibility is to keep before his students hypotheses for thought and action which will fulfill values in the human potential. Where the circumstances change from the time when the hypotheses were offered, these values can serve as the test for human decision.[29] Whether capitalism or communism, for example, dominates the world in the year 2000, the values we should go on pursuing are still those which enhance the unique human powers of the greatest number of people.

V

Capacity to formulate new values and to revise old ones in future history is greater now, especially in this country, than ever before. The peculiar advantages of American settlement in a large and sparsely populated territory, remote from effective military attack, and peopled by culturally advanced pioneers, has been enormous. The availability of learning unrestricted by a monolithic orthodoxy, stratified social and economic classes, and the vast natural resources of the land, have yielded freedom, mobility and individuality envied by much of the civilized world. These special favors of history are being circumscribed now to be sure. As economic interdependence and world communication grow the un-

---

[28]Rene Dubos, "The Despairing Optimist." The American Scholar, 43:1 (Winter, 1973-74), pp. 10-14.
[29]Paul Kurtz, "Education for the Future: The Liberating Arts." In Sidney Hook et. al. (Eds.), The Philosophy of the Curriculum. Buffalo: Prometheus Books, 1975, pp. 201-202.

derdeveloped nations are surely bound for a larger place in the sun.

Nevertheless, "a new type of society" is rapidly taking shape in the Western world where decision about the kind of future we want is coming more and more into our hands. Discretion in arrangement for most of life's values emerges as the great majority of Americans, perhaps a hundred and seventy-five million of them, pass beyond the level of subsistence. Discretionary income despite inflation, and discretionary time beyond working hours, have been built into the core of the nation's culture. Juanita Kreps predicted but a few years ago that by 1985 Americans could work but half a day and half a lifetime without lowering their present standard of living.[30] The present recession lowers that expectation. Yet discretion in social behavior, regardless of age, family, sex, wealth, ethnic background, or vocation is increasing in far-reaching dimensions. Competent aid in decision about these discretionary values looms as a towering need.

Nearly everybody indulges in the sport of prescribing remedies for the future of today's ills. It is crucial for the credible professor to inquire here, as he does about present values to conserve, what basic values are missing that could undergird the future. Pride in "having an angle" or special nostrum for the future is a dangerous goblin to be dispensed. It is the underlying values that make others possible that he must help to find. Are there any critical and irreducibly necessary values to be sought as we work for a sane and humane future?

What could be a more inclusive value essential to future civilization than cultivation of a global conscience? "A world without borders" is perhaps too much to hope for soon. Cultural bias of particular nations and peoples, and the

[30] Phillip Bosserman, Technology Human Values and Leisure. New York: Abingdon Press, 1971, pp. 147, 24.

pride it bespeaks for such representatives, will
and perhaps should remain tap roots of a healthy
civilization. But the cohesion now lacking in
world culture calls for a global ethic in which
the rights of all citizens are respected. The
duty to guarantee them looms as the most fundamental and universal obligation of this age. It
is no mere pious slogan for sky-writing politicians and idealistic clergymen. It is a pressing
practical necessity and a duty intrinsic to the
claims of being a human person, so interrelated
are world-wide cultural forces.

Values in nearly every category have rested
since the beginning of recorded history on the
assumption that man could occupy unclaimed parts
of his environment and transform them to suit his
rational desires. But the admonition of Genesis
(1:28), to "Be fruitful, multiply and replenish
the earth and subdue it," has been endlessly
transformed into disastrous proportions by the
arrival of four billion people on earth. And
this number threatens to double by the year 2000.
The option of accelerating social disruption,
famine, pollution, and epidemics, or formulation
of world-wide obligations to common regulation is
nearing a forced decision.

Efforts by a credible professor to guide
individuals or groups to values in a healthy
and meaningful future will be superficial and
short range unless they rest on some global
perception or master plan into which they can
fit. "Self preservation" is rapidly becoming
a meaningless concept apart from some coordinat-
ing means of relating people that transcends
their political, ethnic, and cultural divisions.[31]
The professor cannot wait for such agencies to be
formed by a kindly providence. Time runs low.

------
[31]Dominique Dubarle, "Critical Aspects of the
Future of the Human Species." In Paul Weiss,
(Ed.), Knowledge in Search of Understanding.
Mount Kisco, N. Y.: Futura Publishing Company,
Inc., 1976, pp. 261-262.

He must couch his teaching in a context that
will encourage such joint efforts of differing people. Consideration of American sover-
eignty, white racial achievements, capitalistic
accomplishments, opportunities provided by its
standard of living, availability of learning,
and similar subjects are all freighted with
overtones about what should be done with "the
other people."

College youth are obviously making up their
minds about the constituents of success, and
some are groping even for "a reason to go on
living." Whatever help a professor gives in
identifying their future values, it needs to
include persuasion that the hedonism underlying the rush to a "better standard of living"
in the West faces an irremovable roadblock
provided by the competing interests of a
world community.

A second task underlying the values that
will ramify through much of future history is
bound to be formulation and support of goals
or ends of technological means. Technology
is basically a means of getting something
done, of reaching a value not yet possessed.
Knowledge of the way to make automobiles or
guns gives the manufacturer an important measure of power over the purchaser of either
product. Economic value accrues to the producer as values of many kinds are released to
the purchaser. A physician by knowledge of
disease acquires power sometimes even of life
or death over patients treated. What ends
should guide the use of such powers?

What is crucial for the future is recognition that use of technological science is a
social matter involving the values in many cases
of large numbers of individuals besides those
employing its powers. Missiles may enrich manu-
facturers of weaponry and shore up at least tem-
porarily the defense of a nation. But they are
obviously designed for destruction of as many
people and their values as they can reach.

Fertilizers yield a profit to the Du Pont Company
and enrich crops, but they often pollute streams
on which fish and wild life depend and cities
rely for drinking water. Cyclamates and fluoro-
carbons are being identified to have similar destructive as well as valuable properties.

Every student of science or user of its
powers should have it indelibly written into
his scheme of values that he has no right to
harm other persons without their consent. Supposition that science is neutral in value, or
intrinsically good and autonomous in its authority, are deadly delusions. "I didn't know
it was loaded," or "What they do with my product
is not my business," simply will not do. Such
belief that one's own values are isolatable
from those of others never was valid, and grows
more vicious daily with accelerating interflow
of social relations. We can find out the out-
come of many technological operations. Not to
do so, or to let them occur as if inherently
"good," is the way of disaster.

Regulation of use, not of scientific inquiry is the great imperative. Except where
the research process itself alters the subject
matter in what could be uncontrollable ways,
such as release of viruses in manipulation of
DNA, inquiry must remain free.[32]   Freedom of
inquiry has earned its right to protection from
every foe. Academia must insist on the cosmic
interpenetration of all values, beginning with
Truth itself, while protecting and assisting
its professors to search in all directions for
new forms of value.

A credible professor will view the recurring reactions against technology by the Rous-
seaus, Nietzsches, Heideggers, Marcuses, and
counter cultural leaders as no wise counsel to

---
[32]Paul Kurtz, "The Ethics of Free Inquiry." In
Sidney Hook and Miro Todorovich, The Ethics of
Teaching and Scientific Research. Buffalo:
Prometheus Books, 1977, pp. 205-206.

return to "the openness of nature." Such advice represents a "failure of nerve" about the role of the intellect in managing human affairs. The poverty and frustration of underdeveloped nations will not go away by a return to "the will of nature" they so far have been unable to fathom. Nor will the confusions and self-defeating enterprises of developed nations, including the dilemma of their relations to underdeveloped ones, be solved by scrapping technology, even if that were possible.

It is recognition of the value import of every scientific venture, and planning for its social use, that is the way of intelligent conduct. Every credible professor can be tested by the way he relates to such an enterprise. For neither he, regardless of his discipline, nor anyone else can avoid involvement in the scientific ventures of this age. Robert Hutchins stated publicly after World War II that he regretted that he had turned over the resources of the University of Chicago to the government and especially to research on the atomic bomb. Such involvement was reprehensible perhaps even more because of its neglect or overshadowing of the social and moral implications of nuclear warfare.

Yet a third valuational thrust for the future essential for a credible professor is the relation of work to values beyond sheer survival, comfort and security. The major contests between the economic systems of the world have always been and will continue to be over the values that labor should be expected to yield. The fact that Americans, comprising five per cent of the world's population, consume over thirty per cent of the earth's resources, indicates that labor in this country is primarily related to the "standard of living" it makes possible. How far will Americans go on at this rate, or be willing to work for the have-not peoples of the earth? That will be a basic test of this country's future as a civilized nation.

114

Who can tell whether capitalism, communism or some other economic system will survive the present worldwide struggle over the role production should play among all the values? The "cultural disjunctions" in capitalism, pointed out by Daniel Bell with renewed clarity,[33] between its stress on efficiency of production, regardless of the way it makes persons "objects" or means to its success, while stressing equality of persons in rights, but still recognizing diversity of talent and the right to individual satisfactions or "fulfillment," do not carry a guarantee of future equilibrium. If economic pluralism is to survive no right can be recognized as absolute. Each must be held subject to common social purposes and made derivative from a super-personal loyalty to the common good.

A Protestant ethic of labor and thrift, to claim divine approval and election, no longer shores up capitalism. The super-American ideal of a "manifest destiny," to capitalize on the unique resources of this new country for the benefit not only of Americans but the entire world, sounds hollow. The development of Russia, China, the Arab countries, and now black Africa, is becoming more and more spectacular. Currently we confront primarily a hedonistic expectation of work in this country. "Full employment" has become an insistent demand upon the American economy. Women must be allowed to work as well as men regardless of their personal or family economic needs. "How much are you making" has become the single most important standard of success, largely because other standards have been less clearly defined or strongly urged.[34]

---

[33] The Cultural Contradictions of Capitalism. New York: Basic Books, Inc., 1976, pp. 11-14, 277-281.

[34] Richard M. Huber, The American Idea of Success. New York: McGraw-Hill Book Company, 1971, p. 451.

My student generation crusaded for "the rights of the working man," which meant to us basically "good working conditions." Today the purposes of work and the adequacy of its rewards make up far more pressing issues. A credible professor will make clear how his discipline will help students "get ahead." And by that phrase he will mean the contribution that their type of "work," whether paid or not, will make to the quality of life. To work for a degree may be as significant as to work for a dollar.

A fourth value interpenetrating so many others is the reliability of rationality itself. Prudent anticipation and planning for the future must be safeguarded from the recurring waste of short-range rescue operations after wars, riots, revolutions, epidemics and similar crises. The fact that planning is so often ineffective in advance of the necessities in a crisis[35] stems not merely from the difficulty of foretelling the future, but in a larger degree from the belief that one must always be "practical." And "practical" usually means some nostrum that "will work" immediately, however irrational.

"A policy of drift attaches only barnacles," as Henry Adams observed.[36] The credible professor seeks to save his students from drift. To do so he will rely on the most useful tool for this task. He will work for the preservation of such a function, not from a presumption of monopoly on wisdom, but from the belief that rationality is crucial to all other values. It assists in the cultivation of many and the understanding of all, for it deals with the import of every experience.

Teaching involves prophecy of what it will be good to know tomorrow. Enmeshed inextricably in this scheme of valuation, the professor worth

---

[35]Dominique Dubarle, op. cit., p. 261, 268.

[36]The Education of Henry Adams. New York: The Modern Library, Inc., 1931, p. 267.

believing is one who understands the value import of his subject and seeks to make those values clear, rationally defensible and promising of endurance.

CHAPTER FIVE

FAUST IN OUR TOWN

I

A professor preparing for class chooses problems in physics, illustrations in literature, issues in economic production or consumption, that are "good enough" to convey to students some import of meaning, and thus some value, worth their remembering. Even in formal subjects like logic, language or mathematics, the signs, words, and other symbols are references of order in the field of raw awareness that have value in making consciousness manageable.

Like Faust in his study, the professor looks for those moments in his subject to which he may say, "Wait, thou art so beautiful." He searches for values worth retention and emphasis. If he ever made a wager with Mephistopheles that there were no such moments in learning, his damnation like that of Faust would be inevitable for his profession would be futile. Consequently, the show-down question for each professor is how he knows that the values he commends deserve such treatment. For the student, the ultimate question is how he knows the values offered by a professor are worth acceptance. In short, what is the test of values that indicates which ones are "good enough" to adopt and recommend?

Such a criterion is the crux of learning for, as we know, values are pivotal in human action as well as thought. Knowledge is no vacant stare at people, places and events, but a scheming perspective on them. It is a way of relating to the world, an anticipation of action or a decision for inaction. One acts when the values in proposed action warrant it. A criterion for values in action figures at every moment, whether conscious or implied.

In an important sense Dr. Gibbs' remark

119

to Mrs. Gibbs in Wilder's play, <u>Our Town</u>, symbolizes the feel for what's good enough to trigger each action. After helping Simon Stimson the village drunk home at midnight, Dr. Gibbs says, "Guess some people ain't made for small town life." He meant that Stimson wasn't good enough for their town. Teaching stems ultimately from some conception of when people are good enough to belong to the human race. A particular discipline is taught as a means of qualifying students for that end.

It is the recognition that criteria of value are often not obvious that leads a student to submit to the rigors of formal instruction. The importance of the professor's standard of legitimacy for feeling good about things must, therefore, be central. Whether he deals with the satisfactions of sense in rock music or Bach, pornography or Rodin, or with the role of intellect and imagination in Milton or Joyce, or the foot pounds of pressure a pier can accept from a cantilever bridge, the professor is concerned with values that are acceptable, either immediately or for longer range satisfactions.

In the dimension of "depth," the direction of scholarship, man plumbs various ranges of his experience with the world. He requires some notion of where his intelligence is heading, and what good his search may hope for, or claim when insight is found. As value is the guide of scholarship, so the competence of the professor to identify, and judge reliably the significance of value stands out as his chief credential.

II

Circumstances where the professor's standard of value is crucial need to be kept in mind. I noticed that professors, like the rest of us, showed their value colors more indelibly during the Vietnam war than at other times. But values require explicit identification regardless of whether a crisis exists.

First of all, the teaching relation itself assumes that students are not yet all they can become. How good should their development be? Whether a subject is descriptive largely, as geology or astronomy, or prescriptive, as in ethics and some phases of political science, learning proceeds toward values not yet thought or possessed. The very process of civilization means pursuit of values deemed essential for a society's future. A professor relies on a standard of what is "better" for his students to know.

After due allowance for freedom of choice by students, respect for differences of opinion, and privacy of judgment, the plain fact remains that the professor's judgment of value should stand in a dominating role. A professor cannot expect "informed consent" to all that he recommends. Students have not yet formed an adequate base of judgment for most of the value ranges in a course. Those taking psychology who turn out to be Freudians, or taking economics, and end by being Keynesians or Marxians and who develop the value perspective of the professor teaching the course, are the surest proof of the pudding. Even if the student takes a different outlook from the professor, he cannot help being aware of the professor's creed. The dynamics of the classroom are such that what the professor considers important figures in the pattern of the course, grades awarded, and the student's development. No matter how "objective" the professor, his criterion of objectivity will show.

A second and more specific circumstance in which the value competence of the professor shows is in the choice of terms considered good enough to "explain" a subject. Concepts are always approximate. Their meaning "spills over the edge" despite refined definition. The term "chair" ranges in meaning all the way from barrel-head to throne as a place to sit. While a value may have a conceptual fuzziness about it too, there is an "immediately found or findable" quality of attraction about it. This attraction has a modal essentiality or un-avoidability about it which attaches to or emerges in all kinds of experience.[1]

A value is no separate dimension, entity, or particle in experience, but a necessary and in-eradicable quality of awareness. Sense experience is attended by modes of color, pitch, hardness or bigness which figure in its comprehension. So the quality of value is a prehension or mode of recognition in consciousness without which "im-portance," "attraction," "true," "belonging," would be senseless reactions. It is such a quality of value that best fits a term which forms the basis of its choice. A "good" term for explana-tion has a stronger appeal than a poor one.

A professor is continuously choosing terms to give "a good explanation." He can never rest with saying the terms he chooses are "representa-tive of the field." He is forced to employ a cri-terion of the values immediately given in them. These terms are valuable and compelling because some intelligible or coherent grasp of things is possible by their use. A good interpretation of Othello's resolve for revenge derives from the interpreting professor's criteria of value for tragic dramas, and ultimately for the lot of man.

Another reason why the credibility of the professor hinges on his standards of value lies in the fact that valuation is directional. It focuses attention of thought, feeling and action by its appeal. Its components of feeling comprise our positive or negative response to a painting, let's say. We like it, are repelled by it, or are content to let it alone. There is a be-havioral component in valuing also, for the value or appeal of an experience ties together various moments of experience which lead to a forth-com-ing action. A cognitive component is involved in these two factors enabling one or another feeling

---

[1] Cf. Clarence I. Lewis, Knowledge and Valuation. La Salle, Ill.: The Open Court Publishing Company, 1946, pp. 365, 401-402.

or action to be judged "better" or "worse."[2]
Since no completely static moment ever exists
in experience, the act of valuation is an assertion of where we are heading. Some criterion
of such directions is essential.

A true cynic could never be a successful
professor. His view that one value is as good
as another would be fatal for intelligence and
decent human social order. Values are "pointers"
for our energies. They call for checks and balances, some standard of "how you know" one or another direction is good enough to pursue. A professor of physics dealing with laser beams reaches
for a standard of direction in thought he takes to
be good, when he explains the nature of such a
beam and its uses. He can no more hold that one
direction is as good as another than a professor
of literature can say one character or literary
usage is as good as another.

Perhaps the fourth occasion when a professor's criteria of value show is the most common,
and the most crucial. The status of value is
central to the distinction of "theoretical" and
"practical" enterprises. How does the professor handle these factors in relation to his discipline? If it is a course in applied psychology, what theories about consciousness, behavior, motivation are held or assumed to be
valid? If the course deals with theory alone
about psychological reactions, what results in
application help to validate it? A course in
advertising based on Skinner's theories of be-
havioristic conditioning would clearly be much
different if rooted in Maslow's views on the
actualization of personality.

Theory and practice are so often distinguished that ideals, the concern of theory, are
separated from values, as if values were only
the interest of practical conduct. But value,
as we have seen, is the attraction of something

---

[2]Cf. Milton Rokeach, The Nature of Human Values.
New York: The Free Press, 1973, p. 7.

"good" in consciousness. To dwell on "ideals"
apart from practice or actual appropriation of
value is to segment conscious experience from
its actual form of occurrence. One attends to
what is taken as "good" in any kind of enterprise. To be an idealist apart from any effort
to realize ideal forms of value is a type of
schizophrenia in attention that fragments arti-
ficially the natural whole of consciousness.

To be sure the values of peace, racial justice, economic opportunity, equality of the sexes
are often embraced by hordes of people who do
nothing to make them effective in human relations.
It is also true that no one can do everything at
once. Critical analysis and justification of
ideal aims may be a full-time occupation at some
periods in every man's life. Many ideals are
habitual, socially conditioned, or formed in ignorance, and require frequent reexamination in
abstraction from actual implementation, and apart
from the risks of their realization.

It is, however, just the willingness to pursue alone either theory or practice, ideal or actual value involvement, independent in each alternative from its corresponding extreme, that frac-
tures our common life. The poles of the earth, it
needs to be remembered, are opposites meaningful
by their reference only to the same planet. Even
in physics, one of the most "theoretical" of all
disciplines, the substance of knowledge consists
in the concepts, definitions, axioms, laws which
provide the ideal, i.e., the best way of dealing
with physical masses and energies.[3] These theoretical constructs are trifling apart from their
polar involvement with man's behavior.

In turning from the delights of classroom
teaching in philosophy to college administration,
I have been instructed by this mutual involvement
of the theoretical and the practical. Conversations with Albert Schweitzer struggling with

---

[3] Werner Heisenberg, Physics and Philosophy. New
York: Harper & Brothers, 1958, p. 108.

tropical disease, Albert Einstein working for
world peace, and Martin Luther King fighting
non-violently for racial justice, have made
this dual concern seem to me remarkable when
held together. Leaders whom we honor are usually masters of this reciprocal involvement.
The atomism of our social disorders and the
segmentation of academia have largely resulted
from scarcity of leaders who have grasped that
one set of values is illegitimate apart from
their involvement with others. Even when values
appear to be opposites, there is frequently some
polar reference that relates them.

III

Despite the pivotal role which hidden or
explicit criteria of values play, many professors are reluctant to pursue them. "It all
seems so vague," they are inclined to say.
Well, what good is it to try to tell when anything _is_ good? Fortunately there are detectable
features of value, I believe, which enable the
professor to judge them reliably.

For one thing, the same value can be observed to perform differing roles and yield different satisfactions in different circumstances.
Judgment of these differences from the sameness
of a value can be trusted when carefully made.
They are shifts in function which can be worked
with intelligibly, just as determination of
temperatures enables one to deal with the function of heat. The most common change in function is the shift from intrinsic to instrumental
value, and vice versa. Health is an elastic
quality good in itself, but instrumental for a
large proportion of accomplishments, and hence
for other values. Money is chiefly instrumental,
though for a numismatist or a miser it may become an end. Music for the orchestra player
may be both enjoyment and a means of livelihood.

Failure to observe these changes in function, or even to be concerned about which function a value serves, are endless sources of con-

fusion and unhappiness. The workaholic who lets his suburban family disintegrate and his health decline, while he tries to go to the top in his company, is the perennial illustration of trying to make instrumental values into intrinsic ones. Massive technological "advances," like food additives, sought independent of the different qualities of life they affect, but supposedly assist, leave the function of their values confused.

Promise of "basic skills" in education, the demand for practical results of learning "so we can get a job," means that emphasis on intrinsic values goes more often by default on the campus than the "how to do it" values. We do well to take to heart Edgar Brightman's observation some time ago that "the fundamental meaning of value is to be found in its intrinsic aspects."[4] Shallowness and failure in life are perhaps more often due to "ignorance of what is good" than "incapacity to achieve it."[5] It is the intrinsic values, the ends we seek, that give meaning to the instruments we use, not the reverse. Our ultimate imperatives come from what matters most intrinsically. It was the centrality of "life, liberty and. . .happiness" which Washington, Jefferson, Adams and the rest made foundational in American history that gave us our national marching orders.

A professor is worth believing who makes clear where values he stresses stand in comparison to each other. He can identify not only their function, he can, secondly, rate their importance. Gradations in value are part of intelligent discourse and hence of meaning. Values are held to be permanent or temporary, limited in range or sweeping in importance, sharply pertinent to a decision or vague and general, higher or lower in quality. Like notes on the scale, they give pitch and quality to each moment of experience, and often affect the perception of each other.

---

[4] Edgar S. Brightman, Nature and Values. New York: Abingdon-Cokesbury Press, 1945, p. 70.

[5] Richard Livingston, Education for a World Adrift. New York: The Macmillan Company, 1945, p. 52.

Who can deny that work, love and holiness are
in an ascending order of value? Work is better
than relief on a dole for it gives self-respect
and independence. The false claimants of welfare
are moral parasites in nearly everybody's book.
Love ranks higher than work because it is less
selfish in motive and less restricted in purpose.
But holiness is higher than either love or work
because it involves one in the ultimate import
of all experience, the total quality of life.
Integral features of value establish these com-
parisons, not mere subjective hopes. There is
apparent here a texture of values. Robert Brown-
ing would say, as in "Paracelsus," that it is reliance on this point-counterpoint of value that
assists man to find his "true purpose, path
and fate."

Disagreement about the priority in rank of
values is to be sure a common cause of conflict.
Violence on the campus in the sixties, expressed
through sit-ins, burning buildings, and riots,
as well as the break-in of Watergate and the resulting cover-ups, stemmed from belief in right-
eous causes. The furor arose in each case from
dissent about which values, whether of civil law,
freedom of speech, justice, or property, even
human life, came first. But this disparity in
opinion must not be allowed to obscure the
fact that values have discernible traits of
quality inherently valid.

Another unmistakable property of values is
their propensity for shrinkage, when pursued
singularly and separate from others. The overwhelming desire to "know thyself" in recent
years has often resulted in decomposition of
identity, as shown in Chapter Two, rather than
fuller grasp of self, as artificial means of
consciousness-raising by means of drugs, sense
control, and various forms of "concentration"
are employed. Fanatical pursuit of "rights"
to everything from employment to homosexuality
and murder, when divorced from duties and institutional authority, is a constant source of turmoil. There are many who point to "the decline

127

of the West" as a consequence of preoccupation
by its NATO powers with their own self-determina-
tion apart from the welfare of the third world.

It is difficult to conceive of a single value
which retains its full strength when taken in abstraction from others. "Honesty," made an absolute
irrespective of qualifying circumstances, comes the
nearest perhaps to such canonization. But even
here a professor can often discourage a student
beyond recovery if he tells him the whole truth
and nothing but the truth about his work. The
fact that such full disclosure of the truth,
sometimes necessary with the lazy or deceitful
student, indicates that the values of time and
the student's motivation condition the value of
truth-telling. The fact remains that "the truth"
is still a value, but its dimensions in the act
of telling are tied up with many other values.

Interrelations among values are typically
difficult to trace, and they vary with circumstances. A change of one component in the
equation shifts the quality of another, as any
effort at "tax reform" by Congress illustrates.
Employment by a mother outside the home raises
her income and self-esteem, but may reduce the
emotional stability and rate of learning by
her child, and hence her quality of motherhood.
But devotion to the ramifications of a subject
will alone remedy the atomism that typifies
our present specialized curriculum. It would
be shameful to admit that only the easily
designated values deserve the attention of
scholars. Let the professor be cheered by
Spinoza's closing sentence to his Ethics:
"All things excellent are as difficult as
they are rare." One price of excellence is
mastery of the problems that arise from membership in patterns which values possess.

Finally there is a time-pertinence which
values manifest. They "fit the times" or not,
as we sense "something is missing," or believe
that the times are not "out of joint." Josiah
Quincy's belief as president of Harvard in 1840

that the wisdom of antiquity "was the essence
of education," since "all essential educational
problems had been solved,"[6] strikes us as strangely
unreal in this experimental age. The generation
gap, notoriously illustrated by parents who assert
that values good enough for them are good enough
for their children, highlights this time factor
in values.

We adjust ourselves to established values,
but also adjust values to the times. "Home" on
a farm in 1900 was much different without television, tractors, airplanes and processed foods.
Being "up-to-date" does not mean adoption of
every new value, but it does mean facility in
judging the bearing of time on values and the
pertinence of values for this time among other
periods in history. Belief that "time will tell"
is an assertion that values have an involvement
with time and that it can be detected.

That values have such discernible features
should save the professor from a romantic expectation, on the one hand, that values take
care of themselves, or a dogmatic claim, on the
other, that his particular values are final.
Characteristics of value are there to be found.
They are tools for use in judgment of what to
do with conceptions of what is good. They are
the components in a criterion necessary to give
values their coherence. If teaching is an art,
and it must be since no two students or professors are alike, the standards of art are crucial
to values in teaching. The professor is a com-
poser to some extent, but a performer mainly, of
valuational music. Notes played vary in tone,
but their quality and relation have harmonic
standards that are reliable.

IV

Since the traits or functions of value are
discernible, the next question concerns the pro-

---

[6]W. H. Cowley, "College and University Teaching,
1858-1958." In Russell M. Cooper (Ed.), The Two
Ends of the Log. Minneapolis: University of
Minnesota Press, 1958, p. 104.

fessor's competence in decision about values to commend. If a professor's valuations are reliable, in what does that reliability consist?

Clearly the first requirement is to observe that values are prior in significance to anything else the professor considers. They are logically prior in importance, if not psychologically prior in origins, to facts, systems, feelings, skills or any other concern the professor may have. They are crucial to all enterprises because the meaning of all enterprises rests with them. To let value considerations go in laboratory or art studio, seminar or lecture is to leave in limbo implements for judging whether anything sensible or important is happening.

Though values have never been detached from any of man's activities, their status has become pressing in proportion to the growing intimacy of human associations and their consequent mutual impingement. Since Darwin the question of what man does to man has grown until human values have become "the dominant philosophic issues of the twentieth century."[7] The role of judgment about value is not merely a logical priority in credible teaching, therefore. It is a question of cultural health and perhaps even of survival.

It is essential to recognize not merely that values deserve to be prior in emphases, but, secondly, that their relation to each other has a primary authority. Walking along a Delaware beach I recently came upon a keel with some bottom planking and side-ribs remaining of what must have been a sailing rigger of some size. My limited knowledge of such vessels prevented me from reconstructing the original character of the ship to which the keel belonged. But a knowledgeable seaman could no doubt conceive it with almost complete accuracy. Experiences of value call for pursuit of the rest of the story. They have an ancestry and family

---

[7] John A. Irving, Science and Value. Toronto: Ryerson Press, 1952, p. 138.

membership that attest to their claim for acceptance. They are parts of a meaningful whole the
comprehension of which accounts for their appeal.

Only totalities can be meaningfully analyzed.
An item that is a complete orphan in experience
could not even be identified, as gestalt psychologists have established. We grasp value as a
feature of awareness by reference to "what it belongs to," what it is like or unlike. Each Er-
lebnis belongs to one's Erfahrung, in which connections with other meaningful complexes exist,
as the Germans would say. Drinking water when
thirsty is considered "good" because it relates
to other experiences of satisfaction when such
a liquid is swallowed.

Value in abortion, for example, can not be
responsibly dealt with apart from a wide-ranging
scheme of values. Relief from an unwanted pregnancy may be of the greatest importance where
health of the woman, or known deformity of the
child, are at stake. Incest and rape could per-
petuate the degradation of both parents as well
as the child unless the fetus is aborted. But
when abortion is approved on request of the
pregnant woman, irrespective of circumstances,
it may mean also approval of unrestrained and
casual intercourse. To expect the state to pay
for abortions sought by the poor, when no necessity of health presses, or moral complications
of rape or incest arise, is to expect subsidy of
sexual liberty. A woman deserves "control of
her own body," as abortionists say, but that
control can be expected to result in avoidance
of pregnancy also.

A professor concerned with James Joyce's
Ulysses can profitably assist students to find
the images, dreams, motives and other fragments
that float through the "existential moments" in
the stream of consciousness. There is value in
recognition of such factors. It is a type of
art that highlights "the way things are." But
such disintegration of the wholeness in experience necessary to manage one's life can only be
a shallow value. It is a temporary analysis de-

131

pendent upon a larger grasp of human valuation for its significance. A professor of English who told me he regards Joyce as the most outstanding writer of the twentieth century, surely can't have a thorough comprehension of the value references implicit in literature as an art.

Choice of values in their simple circumstances usually presents little difficulty. It is their ramifications in differing circumstances, their affinities and differences, that are critical. "Equal education" was long an obvious value to be supported by American democracy. But the implication of "separate but equal" did not become a recognized national hazard until 1954. Racial purity and vigor arouses loyalty and self-respect, both solid values. But the interface of races adamant in adherence to these values has meant murder of Jews in Germany, Palestinians and Jews in the Middle East.

Where the professor is needed most is where values lead. He needs to be competent in handling their intersection. Perhaps the most critical part of his work consists in tracing out and interpreting the interpenetration and gradation of values. He is a specialist in showing the value implications in options, whether he deals with economic, political, religious, artistic, or indeed any other kind of question.

A third requirement for adequacy in dealing with value factors is regular and articulate regard for the parameters of valuation. Neglect of any one of four such constants and disregard of their mutual involvement warps the process of value judgment.

Nature, both in its space-time form and in the logically given conditions of order in thought, provides a habitat for man in relation to which values play a role. Such a structure to things with its persisting features provides conditions for a life-span in which some experiences are better than others. The significance of man's life is judged in relation to these given factors, some of which he can modify, but all of which figure in his destiny. Naturalists, idealists, and meliorists play up or down the role of nature in the "success" of one's life. The central factor is that values are always properties of man's relation to some feature or features of nature which are independent of his own thought, and prior to his existence. He shapes his destiny, or is shaped by it in relation to given conditions.

Persistence and eminence of a human self as a recipient and benefactor of the valuing process combine as a second ingredient for intelligible valuation. Attacks on the integrity and wholeness of the self by modernist writers, such as Samuel Beckett, are themselves unintelligible apart from an enduring self that gathers critical factors into its judgments. It is neglect of human persons as ends in themselves, the focus of valuation, as Kant emphasized, which vitiates the value process and undermines social intercourse. Workers as means to the profit of factory owners, apart from their desert of healthful working conditions and a decent wage, are victims of disvalue. Values are not free-swinging entities in the atmosphere, but qualities of man's interaction with nature and other human beings.

This focus of value in persons carries with it some "community" of value properties by which people understand each other's aims and satisfactions. The same values can be recognized in similar and to some extent in differing circumstances. "Lies is lies," no matter what the circumstances, was Joe Gargery's emphatic message to Pip in Great Expectations. Persons can identify, compare, communicate recognizable values to each other. Persons with some common value experiences are the assumption of a civilized society. The stress on "alienation" and "disillusionment" of much current scholarship shows unwillingness to rely on this feature of shared valuations, which is undeniably available. Actually, apart from common features of value, such a generalization about the utter privacy "alienation" reflects would itself be impossible.

A third parameter emerges inevitably from the second, namely the rational power of man to tran-

scend, and to form judgments of value about many
of the natural and social forces that play upon
them. Even the Nietzsches who affirm that dependable values are arrived at non-rationally,
or super-rationally, "explain" their decisions
and try to justify them. Valuation is an affirmation that an attitude, feeling, or action is sensible or reasonable enough to reach for and assert.
Unless valuation has sufficient cognitive powers
to transcend temperamental idiosyncrasies, the
peculiarities of individual past conditioning,
and the individual features of differing objects
in the environment, intelligent action would be
impossible. We could not otherwise learn from
experience or improve our lot. We could not even
do harm to others, for such actions presume a
rational judgment of value or disvalue.

A fourth parameter of valuation is the institutional reference values inevitably possess. In
my first college class in sociology the professor
urged us to write on the flyleaf of our text book,
"Human nature develops within and decays outside
of social relations." This axiom about the extension, protection and growth of personality means
that the values affirmed by anyone are the preferences of a familial, political, religious, economic, and artistic individual. What we take to
be good is enmeshed in the institutions in which
we and others participate for we cannot escape them.
A "good day's work" is an activity in a pattern of
employment affected by those who make it possible,
share in it, and benefit from it.

Adam and Eve discovered jointly, distinctions
in value represented by the tree of life. It was
a family affair. Critical value choices about
property, children, civil power, worship are about
the goodness or badness of participation in social
institutions with a reputation for fostering or
hindering values that are cherished. Submergence,
subversion, transformance, or transcendence of institutions are frontiers on which judgments of
value are daily formed. It is on these frontiers
that the professor's skill in value formation is
badly needed. He must know his institutions! The

criteria of scientific maturity are perhaps more clearly recognized as joint, and institutionally established than those of the humanities. But all ranges of culture have such institutional reference.[8]

V

A credible professor looks to the intricate involvement of values with each other and to the factors which frustrate them. Competence in knowing a value when you see one is of course a major task in this mechanized society. But the clash of values daily experienced is the source of crises in culture and the turning points where professorial competence is most needed.

Even to assert a value is to conflict with something to avoid. A good apple may be eaten while a rotten one is to be thrown away. This is not to say that every good has a corresponding evil. But embracing one good may displace, limit, or supersede another. A value represents a matching of human reactions with the way things are, a harmony with the scheme of things at their best. Cancer, a frustration of value, represents some disharmony not yet understood between health habits and the requirements of the organic world. Murder violates the value of life claimed by the victim because a "better" value is sought however blindly by the assailant.

Belief in a value is an assertion of legitimacy, an affirmation that a good will arise when sought, despite competition from other interests, whether my own or another's. We crave a reliability in these options chosen. The natural tendency is to look for simplistic, absolutely reliable answers to competing claims, whether they have to do with the amount of alcohol to drink on New Year's eve or the obligation to pay back a bank loan.

---

[8]Cf. Martin Green, "The Visible College in British Science." The American Scholar, 47:1 (Winter, 1977-78), p. 114.

A charge of dogmatism, rigidity, stubbornness
easily arises when a value is defended as "final."
On the other hand, indifference to the fate of
values is an invitation to confusion, qualitative
degeneration in life, and ultimately to despair.
We tend to admire Joan of Arc with her certain
voices, while our own uncertain values remain less
vivid than we wish. At the same time, the value
flux of skid row seems a catastrophe we must not
allow our vagueness to reach. Adjudication between
these extremes comprises the cutting edge of our
value ventures.

Most crucial decisions about values are polar.
They are conclusions about contrary thrusts toward value, either of which would be productive,
but not attainable independent of its polar opposite. Most values stand in tension with each other.
Competence in handling this tension is the ultimate
task of the professor. His credibility comes at
last to his ability to perform this eventual task
of all thinkers.

Ultimate problems of economics are polar.
Capitalism construes it to be in the public interest to produce efficiently, conserve resources,
reward workers equitably and meet the needs of
private comfort and security as far as profit and
efficiency allow. On the other hand, it encourages
the private interest in full employment at high
wages, increase in personal development, and extension of private satisfactions. Since communism
locates the balance closer to the public interest
and capitalism closer to private interests, any
professor dealing with economic questions reckons
willy-nilly with this polar relation.[9]

Business policy is inevitably a balance of
contraries neither extreme of which contains the
criterion of its own adequacy.[10]   A buyer adjusts

---

[9]Cf. Daniel Bell, The Cultural Contradictions of
Capitalism. New York: Basic Books, Inc., Publishers, 1976, Chap. I.

[10]Cf. Sir Geoffrey Vickers, The Art of Judgment.
New York: Basic Books, 1965.

the flow of materials into his store according to the rate by which they flow out. His decisions are based on the probable consumption of goods resulting from the confluence of many variables among purchasers, and the quality, availability, and responsiveness of suppliers. Policies are "good enough" so long as competition is not cutthroat or collusion exploitative, jobs are secure but featherbedding is avoided, workers are safeguarded, but profits are preserved.

A navigator for an airplane calculates the confluence of air currents, pressures, and gravitational pulls that will allow the ship to reach a destination valued above others for a given flight. The formulae of these variables are juxtaposed in such a way as to enable the craft to maneuver up or down, right or left. A psychologist is calculating the physiological, and also the non-spatial "mental," phenomena that make up consciousness, when studying man. A sociologist or political scientist is concerned with the individual qualities of satisfaction persons seek in relation to contrary social and political forces affecting them.

It is safe to say that man's "quest for certainty," as John Dewey named the desire for dependable values, turns out to be a quest for capacity to navigate in the presence of contrary value claims. Henry Novotny advises that an ethical, or credible, professor should be more concerned with conflict resolution than with advocacy of any one value taken as absolute.[11] The desire for "transcendent values," so widespread in today's popular "meditation" groups, expresses a feel after skill in reconciling the polar tensions central in all experience.

Is there any more ultimate service a professor can render to a student than to provide some means of dealing with inevitable tensions in the polarities among values? Twenty years after publishing a

---

[11]"Objectivity and Biased Skepticism in Higher Education." In Sidney Hook, et. al. (Eds.), The Ethics of Teaching and Scientific Research. Buffalo: Prometheus Books, 1977, p. 61.

book on this task, and at the end of forty years
of struggle with contrary values in learning both
as professor and administrator, I have found none.[12]

When Kant came to the end of his classic
critique of reason's power to know "things-in-
themselves," he concluded that "practical reason," as distinguished from "pure reason," must
make postulates with which we proceed, if intelligence of any kind is to be preserved. As we
try to make sense of our lives we have no choice
but to postulate the ideals of thought, the most
valuable projection of directions to take in
thought and action. The texture of these valuations, which we may call the "architectonic of
values" in place of Kant's "architectonic of reason," is the ultimate tool of a scholar's workshop.
And it consists in the devices he uses to deal
with the polarities among values.

A few illustrations of such devices may be
instructive. There is what I have called the
principle of polar autonomy. For values to be
meaningful they must have some life of their own,
a peculiar capacity to nourish human need in a
unique way. When pushed to an extreme, however,
as in free sex, political freedom in the form of
anarchy, tolerance of religion to the degree of
atheism, the limits of a value appear. It is
lack of imagination to conceive and will power
to pull back from the limits in values that bring
on disaster. Any value chosen must be required
to show credentials of where it will lead. Though
we do not always know where a clear value will
eventually lead, its full range, limit and circum-
ference are questions whose answers help us to deal
with it. They should be constantly pressed.

Attention to what may be called polar aug-
mentation is a second useful principle. The extent to which each pole in a value dilemma is involved in its opposite can be a source of insight
into the management of each. Each blade of the

---

[12]For details consult my _Polarity, A Philosophy of Tensions
Among Values_. Chicago: Henry Regnery, 1957, Chap. I,
"A Calculus for Polarity."

scissors performs its function by moving in opposite direction from its companion. As science
stresses more and more the changes, energy or
processes in nature, the more the structural per-
manencies, e.g. the laws of valence and quantum
mechanics, become apparent. Growth in organisms
is possible only as the persistence of certain
constants, cell relations, or "forms" are maintained. Advanced countries assist developing
countries to flower, but further their own health
through resulting expansion in employment and
growth in markets. Liberty of individuals is
ultimately preserved by surrender of some of its
ranges to control by civil government.

In the physical sciences the ratio between
polar factors can often be given a mathematical
formula. Such equations of balance are not so
attainable in psychological or social sciences
or in the arts and humanities. Nevertheless,
the role of contrapletion by one pole of its
contrary companion's function is a fertile means
of value management. Originality in musical
composition, for example, can be judged by its
use of "standard" or basic tonal forms. New and
old forms of sound have an inevitable involvement
with each other.

Perhaps the most inescapable process in valuation is the principle of organic concretion. Each
thought we have is "singular" and unique, an occurrence in a fragmentary moment of universal time.
But it is the membership of this moment in some
meaningful whole that is the source of its intel-
ligibility. It is the resolution of diversities
among objects, events, and hence among values that
constitutes mental equilibrium. For the truth, as
Karl Jaspers insisted, "has coherence, the false
is scattered."13   An integrated personality deals
successfully with conflicts in value by reference
to the intelligible whole to which each particular
value belongs. The resting place of thought about
the contrary thrust of values that is taken to be

13The Perennial Scope of Philosophy. New York:
The Philosophical Library, 1949, p. 147.

"good enough" may be rational order, aesthetic
balance, psychological adjustment, emotional fulfillment, or all of these together. The point is
that some "transcendent" whole is inevitably in-
voked as the frame of meaning to which each value
is referred, when its "significance" is considered.

A credible professor develops the value implications of his subject and assists his students to
manage them. The conflicts among values allow some
degree of management in ways so often neglected.
The important mark of the reliable professor is
that he does not abandon the fate of values to the
autonomy of nature, the whim of immature preferences by students, the determinism of history, or
pressure of vested interests. He carries responsibility for the cultivation, organization and
recommendation of values above that of any other
member of his society.

VI

If the academic community is to halt the retreat from education and restore the credibility
of its professors, some major even drastic changes
will have to be made in the qualification of professors. Change in the standards of excellence
and in the rewards provided are in order. The
traditional views that values do not belong in
reliable scholarship, or if they do they will
take care of themselves, are simply obsolete.
To suppose that values of students will change
for the better willy-nilly by virtue of a college
education, even in a church-related institution,
is naive.

Preparation for adequacy in dealing with
values cannot be expected from the Ph.D., the
usual union card for a typical professor. The
accuracy in research and thoroughness in problem-
solving that this degree represents has, of course,
long since justified it as essential for a professor in most fields. Until and unless a professor
has proved to the satisfaction of competent authorities that he knows how to go about investigat-
ing a scholarly problem, any further activity of

his may well be superficial. The problem lies
with factors the degree falls short in providing.

As Chairman of a committee for a half dozen
years in the Association of American Colleges on
the preparation of the professor, I joined in in-
numerable conferences on the subject. Alternative degrees, such as the doctor of arts, seem
always to skirt the incisiveness that scholarship requires. The vogue of post-doctoral studies
now current serves more commonly to mean some further specialization in the original discipline,
rather than development of competence in valuation.
Conditional validity to a Ph.D. for a limited
period of ten years, until updated by further
graduate work, as suggested for the sciences,[14]
would mean more of the same specialization apart
from values.

Conversations and seminars with the Council
of Graduate Schools, lead me to conclude that the
graduate deans are commonly stymied in their hopes
for changes in graduate study by the entrenched
department chairmen under their supposed direction. The momentum of "established" scholars
in the departments and the autonomy provided by
outside funds, at least until recent months, have
defined grooves that make it unlikely that any
other preparation of professors will be supported
in the foreseeable future. Unfortunately, this
leaves the completion of the professor's preparation to the employing institution for on-the-job
training.

Delegation of "value studies" to philosophy
departments bears little promise of remedy for
the deficit in valuational competence the typical
academic community manifests. In the first place,
the vogue of electives means that few students
relatively speaking take any courses in philosophy. Still fewer go beyond preliminary stages
where many philosophical concepts remain forbid-
ding and esoteric. Secondly, such separate and
segmented study of values leaves the question of

---

[14]Caryl P. Haskins, "Thoughts on an Uncharted Future."
In Paul Weiss, op. cit., p. 245.

141

value import in other departments for the clumsy application by a student to the rest of his studies. The result is bound to be uneven and often negligible.

What is even more serious is that departments of philosophy have so commonly been playing down value studies.[15] Preoccupation with linguistic analysis, scientific methodologies, and forms of logical empiricism that render values "emotive" and largely fictional, has seriously restricted the contribution of the philosophy departments to the value life of instruction in many institutions. Wittgenstein's pronouncement that "you can at best stammer when you talk about them [i.e., values]" has been a pontification with devastating results. Some students have been gaining in desperation what value sustenance they can from studies in anthropology, sociology and literature. Assistance by these courses is to the credit of their professors but it remains sporadic and unsystematic.

It follows from the study of values set forth in these pages that concern for the value import of every subject treated is the business of each professor. The dichotomy is false between "liberal" and "professional" courses, theoretical and applied studies. Meaning in any study has value in its integral structure. Mastery of any subject requires attention to the nature and import of values with which one takes that study to be "good enough" to pursue and utilize. Whitehead's view of education as "the art of utilization of knowledge"[16] should not be taken as a separate operation after ideas are acquired. It is the very participation of values in our grasp of what is important to respond to, that directs our next move.

---

[15]Cf. Martin Marty, "Whatever Happened to Philosophy?" Saturday Review, Dec. 10, 1977, p. 31; Taylor Branch, "New Frontiers in American Philosophy." The New York Times Magazine, Aug. 14, 1977, pp. 12 ff.
[16]Op. cit., p. 16.

Such articulation of the value import in each discipline calls for some such competence in dealing with value as I have outlined above. But few professors commonly possess such an outlook, or facility in its implementation if they sought it. Since the preparation for college teaching cannot be expected to supply such competence, and the momentum of present goals of scholarship verge in other directions, some different source of emphasis on values in learning will have to be found.

This brings us to the keepers of the seal of academic life, the trustees and administrators of the supposed goals of higher learning. At present these custodians of learning are administering so often a reward system that undermines the very integrity of the undertaking for which they are responsible. Faculty members as professional educators usually interpret the goals of the institution in their own way, and sometimes seek even to determine the stated goals, or even the charter, of the institution. The result is the present segmented, value-indifferent, or confused curriculum which even many of them lament.

Many a college president has lost his health or resigned (363, or 12 per cent of those in office in 1976) because of the irreconcilable expectations of leadership and the diverging forces of faculty, students, alumni and supporters which prevent coordination, say nothing of leadership. The present sagging support of higher education must certainly be related to this chaotic condition. After eighteen years in the president's chair, I see no solution except a new demand by college authorities that their employees develop competence in valuation. This means the capacity to understand the direction their teachings lead, and the will to seek an intelligent and meaningful relation among the values their institution seeks.

Faculty committees, generally on the ground of "academic freedom," resist administrative pres-

143

sure for educational reform.[17]   Efforts at "faculty renewal," such as those reported by Jerry Gaff,[18] are usually looked upon by faculty members with mild enthusiasm. So casual in importance do they seem that faculty members characteristically seek to persuade administrators to support them only with "soft" money, and devote regular and reliable funds to support their conventional procedures of teaching.

The only choice before administrative officers is to allow this disastrous condition to continue, or to take seriously their commission as custodians of "reliable education" and insist on a new approach to values in learning. With the leveling off of college enrollments, and future decline in prospect, an increasing per cent of faculty members is becoming tenured. The obligation of the institution to aid further growth of present faculty members rests with its administrators. Though faculty members dislike the connotation of "renewal," "retooling," "upgrading," they can be led to help plan for such comprehensive reform, when their views are consulted and participation is rewarded.

It would be impossible to prescribe a uniform program for differing institutions of course. Whether seminars in value theory for faculty members, interdisciplinary collaboration in courses, sabbatical studies of the value-implications in specific disciplines, value inventories of curricula, value autobiographies by each professor, or

---

[17] Arthur Bestor insists that faculty members must "refuse to accept as permanent. . .alterations in curriculum and governance" planned by trustees and administrators "without genuine faculty deliberation and unambiguous faculty approval." "In Defense of Intellectual Integrity." In Sidney Hook, et. al. (Eds.), The Modern Idea of a University, op. cit., p. 63.

[18] Toward Faculty Renewal. San Francisco: Jossey-Bass, Publishers, 1976, Chap. II.

similar devices are chosen is of secondary importance. What is primary is that specific address of value ramifications of each discipline
by each teacher be induced and growth in "value
competence" be insisted on.

Preparation of a faculty to deal adequately
with value questions is an expensive undertaking.
It requires "hard money" to free professors from
some responsibilities in teaching, administration and research. But it is a sober fact that
many present expenditures are not getting the
right results. The reports from the Cooperative
Institutional Research Program, begun in 1966
and carried out by the American Council on Education and the University of California at Los
Angeles, are seriously critical of how funds in
higher education are being spent. Over the
past decade a sampling of more than 300 institutions and an accumulation of data on some 200,000
students show that policy in American higher education is being shaped by "economic considerations" more than by "enhancing student progress."[19]
Income from enough "full time equivalent" students
determines so many crucial educational questions.

Complaints about the costs of higher education would surely not be so great if it were
clear that they were incurred for the right ends.
And what ends are greater than the value competence of the professors? Remodeling what we are
doing with hard money is our task, not adding on
some questionable frill.

As the turmoil of the '60s reached its mighty
crescendo the organization of "University Centers
for Rational Alternatives" took place. Among its
notable publications The Idea of a Modern University
has apparently been an effort to show what the present university should be doing. Its title is obviously offered in place of Cardinal Newman's plan
for St. Andrews in the early 1850s. But instead
of any cohesive scheme to replace the confusion

---

[19]Alexander W. Astin, Four Critical Years. San
Francisco: Jossey-Bass, Publishers, 1977, p. x,
et passim.

that prevails, it is largely a defense, often peevish, of the disjointed multiversity. It ends with a flourish in John Searle's recommendation that "boards of trustees should be abolished" and administrators made "the arm of the faculty. . ."[20]

But the lowest common denominator, typical of faculty reports, will not save the academic community from disaster. Concentration on values of what learning can become will save it. Newman's belief that knowledge brings a "sense of enlargement" bearing "an intrinsic fecundity" was a true insight, for it refers to something "found" that is important, not invented. It breaks in to a story with more to come. Awareness of a single particular is not "knowledge." It consists in "a connected view" of things and as such is "its own end."[21] The value import of any perspective leads to implications which enable the learner to decide what is "good enough" to respond to and remember.

Values belong to meaning and can serve as the focus of the learning community. They give more promise of reconciling the diversities in scholarship than any other device, for they are relatively limited in number. Their "goodness," and therefore appeal, rests in an important sense in their unification of diverging particulars in experience, as Plato saw. Left to follow their own specialties, faculty members will not transform academia into the community its own health requires. I reach this conclusion with sadness since I have always tried to preserve my early outlook as a professor before becoming an administrator.

No imposition of a preconceived orthodoxy, fixed scheme of indoctrination, or platform of an ecclesiastical body, or political party need be supposed in such a recommendation. Parochialism in all its forms is outmoded in most areas of the "free" world. The indoctrination of totalitarian countries is a retrogression in cultural

---

[20]Ibid., p. 281-282.

[21]John Henry Cardinal Newman, The Idea of a University, (Ed. Svaglic). New York: Rinehart & Company, Inc., 1960, pp. 101, 84, 77.

health, and resistance to it here and there even in communistic countries raises the question of how long it can maintain itself. But uniform emphasis upon the process of valuation is an entirely different thing from demand for uniformity of conclusions. There is an integrity about values that constitutes their own authority. The important thing is for professors and students to learn how to find them and to follow their meaningful refer- ences. They comprise the thread of Theseus to lead us out of our labyrinth of confusing desires.

151

152

Truth (continued) 49, 50,
  54, 61, 76, 77, 81, 87,
  104, 113, 128, 139

Value, 4, 5, 8, 13;
  Christian, 24, 25-26,
  36, 60, 119;
  criterion, 119-120, 122,
  129; definition, 12-13;
  instrumental, 125;
  intrinsic, 125-126, 153;
  plurality, 24; types,
  13-15
Van Leer, O., 52
Vickers, G., 158
Vocation: professor's,
  9, 34, 41, 42, 56,
  60, 61
Vocationalism, 28-29, 52,
  61

Weber, M., ix
Weiss, P., 46, 52, 77,
  111, 141
Wells, H. G., ix
Werdell, P., 95
Wesley, J., 80
Whitehead, A. N., 27, 40,
  82, 142
Whitman, W., 38, 39-40,
  55
Wilder, T., 120
Wilson, W., 77
Wittgenstein, L., 142
Wolfe, T., 80
Wordsworth, 47
Work, 25, 97, 98, 114,
  127

Young, J. A., 42

ABOUT THE AUTHOR

A graduate of Otterbein College, Dr. Norris did his graduate work at Boston University, Harvard and the University of Berlin, just prior to the Hitler era. He taught philosophy for several years at Baldwin-Wallace College and DePauw University. He also served respectively as vice-president and dean of the faculty for a part of the time during appointment at these institutions.

Eighteen years were spent as a college president, first at MacMurray College and then at Albion College. As a member of the Association of American Colleges, he served as chairman for some time of the committee on preparation of college professors. After retirement from Albion College, Dr. Norris became a program officer, and for a time director of the division of education, at the National Endowment for the Humanities. In this capacity, he interviewed hundreds of professors and studied programs in humanities on many campuses from coast to coast. He has also served as Lecturer and Advisor in Humanities at George Washington University.

Recipient of several honorary degrees, he is a member of Phi Beta Kappa and received an award for contributions to higher education from the International Association of College and University Presidents.